MUSICOLOGY IN THE 1980s

Methods, Goals, Opportunities

Da Capo Press Music Series

EXECUTIVE EDITOR
BEA FRIEDLAND
Ph.D., City University of New York

MUSICOLOGY IN THE 1980s
Methods, Goals, Opportunities

Edited by
D. Kern Holoman
and
Claude V. Palisca

DA CAPO PRESS • NEW YORK • 1982

Library of Congress Cataloging in Publication Data

Main entry under title:

Musicology in the 1980s.

(Da Capo Press music series)
Proceedings of 2 panels held at the fall 1981 meeting of the American Musicological Society in Boston.
Contents: Musicology I: Methodology, opportunities and limitations. Editor's
introduction/Claude V. Palisca. Reflections on musical scholarship in the
1960s/Claude V. Palisca. Archival research/Jeremy Noble. [etc.]
1. Musicology—Addresses, essays, lectures. I. Holoman, D. Kern, 1947-
II. Palisca, Claude V.
ML3797.1.M877 1982   780′.01   82-14966

Proceedings of two panel sessions—Musicology I ("Current Methodology") and
Musicology II ("The Musicologist Today and in the Future")—held during the
American Musicological Society meeting in Boston, November 12–15, 1981.
Some portions of this book are in copyright and used here with permission;
acknowledgments will be found at appropriate places in the text.

Published by Da Capo Press, Inc.
A Subsidiary of Plenum Publishing Corporation
233 Spring Street, New York, N.Y. 10013

Publisher's Preface

This volume comprises the proceedings of the two panels chaired, respectively, by Claude V. Palisca and D. Kern Holoman—sessions informally known as *Musicology I* and *Musicology II*—at the Fall 1981 meeting of the American Musicological Society in Boston. The papers at these panels, conceived by the convention Program Committee as thoughtful reviews of musicology's current state along with judicious forecasts of its future, eventuated as a series of stimulating, no-holds-barred critiques, caveats, and proposals for change. The ideas of both the seasoned authorities of Palisca's Methodology panel and the Second Wave activist-scholars in Holoman's group fostered the kind of keen listening and lively discussion that are the hoped-for goals—hoped-for, but not always achieved—of all scholarly intercourse.

There was nothing for it but to publish the papers from both sessions

5

and make them available not only to the musicological community at large but to performers, critics, and people in related fields. In preparation for the present volume, all the participants revised/expanded/ footnoted the original spoken words as necessary for publication, and the two chairmen-turned-editors have produced introductions to their particular segments of the book. Moreover, an important article by Claude Palisca, first published in 1978 as part of a major UNESCO project in the humanities, is included here as an appropriate framework for the deliberations of the Boston panelists.

The designation "co-editors" hardly describes the actual role of the chairmen in making this edition a reality. Working with their panel colleagues during the early stages, they each demonstrated uncommon diplomatic and organizing skills, essential qualities in an enterprise involving ten busy, strong-minded academics. Then, with characteristic exuberance and flair, Kern Holoman tried-and-erred until he mastered, in record time, the arcana of computerized wordprocessing and composition on brand-new equipment; this feat was a *sine qua non* for our collaborative undertaking. And with *his* distinctive erudition, zeal, and low-key humor, Claude Palisca passed his critical eye over the full set of proofs.

Withal, these prodigious labors alone could not have created a proper book — let alone an attractive one — without the careful and ingenious ministrations of Karen Brooks, Da Capo's senior artist and book designer.

Finally, a personal note in respect to the two editors. The resonant and bracing triad formed in the course of our extended New York-New Haven-Davis dialogue has been and continues to be a veritable tonic: firm, and altogether harmonious.

                                                              —Bea Friedland

Contents

7

Musicology II

THE MUSICOLOGIST
TODAY AND IN THE FUTURE

Musicology I

CURRENT METHODOLOGY
Opportunities and Limitations

Editor's Introduction

The initiative for this panel discussion came from the Program Committee for the 1981 meeting in Boston of the American Musicological Society and its chairman, Jeffrey Kurtzman, who invited me to organize a review of the current state and trends in this discipline. I first thought of naming it: "Musicology since *Musicology*," slyly recalling that other survey of the state of the field, as of around 1960, in which Frank Harrison, Mantle Hood, and I collaborated.

The invitation to organize this panel was almost to be expected: I have been doing penance for my sins of omission and failures of prophetic vision regularly every ten years since my essay in that publication. Ten years ago UNESCO asked me to prepare the section on music in the mammoth study, *Main Trends of Research in the Social and Human Sciences,* part 2, published finally in English and French in

11

1978. I mention this because anyone reading my two essays will easily conclude that the forward-looking trends I identified have mostly evaporated. I have utterly failed at divination. The UNESCO study has been reprinted here for those who wish to verify this observation. Also, it promised to be useful in a book that surveys the field as of the early 1980s to have as a background a panoramic view from the vantage point of the early 1970s.

Some of the trends I thought promising in 1970 were: the application of ethnomusicological method to historical studies of western music, that is, looking at how music functions in all levels of a culture; another was new theories of musical structure, such as those of Milton Babbitt and Allen Forte; or computer applications in analysis, bibliography, and thematic listing; and the diffusion of musicological findings through contact with the elementary and secondary schools and the public media. It is significant that none of these appear on the present agenda. Musicology advances (if Leo Treitler will permit me that verb) in unpredictable ways.

As I reviewed the periodicals and books of the last ten years, what impressed me were not novel methodologies but the intensified and more critical exploitation of some traditional ways of doing scholarship: regional archival studies that attempt to reconstruct in depth entire musical cultures (if not in an ethnomusicological fashion); renewed efforts to establish links with the history of thought and with particular strains in it, such as rhetoric; a return to sketches and autographs as evidence of the process of musical creation; after waves of Schenker and Babbitt, a search for historically valid, multilateral, and contextual approaches to analysis; and a more critical use than heretofore of pictorial evidence as a source for musicological information.

I invited to join the panel some of the leading scholars identified with these trends. I asked them to present, not so much theoretical exposition of methods, as critical assessment of the significance of what has been done with them, and their potential for the future. Some of the questions I suggested they might address were the following. How has the methodology contributed to our understanding of the music and musical cultures of the past? What are some examples of successful application and some less so? In what directions do these applications seem to be pointing the discipline? What are some of the limitations of the method? I was gratified that the particular scholars I asked, themselves very active in current research in the subdisciplines of which they spoke, took time out to consider these questions and to frame their thoughts for the rest of us to contemplate.

The presentations were followed by both prepared and impromptu responses. Because no published report of the panel's deliberation was projected, no record was made of it. Some of the panelists took the discussion into account, however, in revising their statements, so we are grateful to those who participated: Roy Wates and James Haar, who responded to Rika Maniates; Richard Kramer, to Joseph Kerman; and Richard Leppert, Colin Slim, and Tilman Seebass, to James McKinnon.

—Claude V. Palisca

The following article is reprinted from a UNESCO study: Section III, "Music," by Claude V. Palisca from Chapter V, "Contemporary Study of the Principal Problems in Aesthetics and the Various Arts," by Mikel Dufrenne *et al.*, from Part Two, *Main Trends of Research in the Social and Human Sciences,* Volume One: *Anthropological and Historical Sciences, Aesthetics and the Sciences of Art,* ed. Jacques Havet (The Hague, Paris, New York: Mouton Publishers/UNESCO, 1978), pp. 791-802. It is reproduced by permission of UNESCO.

Reflections on Musical Scholarship in the 1960s

Claude V. Palisca

The study of music, of all the arts, is the most difficult to circumscribe as a discipline. As soon as scholars probe its problems with any depth, it spills into neighboring fields—social and physical sciences, philosophy, literature, and history. It is easier to identify musicologists than to define musicology.

The founders of musicology saw it as a universal science, and called it *Musikwissenschaft*. Karl Friedrich Chrysander (1826-1901) wished to see it modeled on the exact sciences. Reflecting this ideal, Hugo Riemann (1849-1919), a professor at Leipzig, conceived the field as containing five divisions:[1] (1) acoustics, (2) tone-physiology and-

[1] Hugo Riemann, *Grundriss der Musikwissenschaft* (1908; 4th edn., ed. Johannes Wolf, Leipzig 1928).

Claude V. Palisca is Henry L. and Lucy G. Moses Professor of Music, Yale University.

psychology, (3) musical aesthetics, including speculative music theory, (4) theory of composition or performance, and (5) music history.

In a number of German universities today, for example in Hamburg, Cologne, and at Humboldt-University in Berlin, all of these branches of musical study are still included in institutes of musicology. A number of such institutes exist also elsewhere, for example in Warsaw, Ljubljana, Moscow, and Tokyo. In England, France, and Italy, which, with the United States and Germany, are the leading countries in musical scholarship, university musical studies consist chiefly of theory, criticism, and the history of Western music.

From the standpoint of what musicologists actually do, then, the field appears more restrictive than traditional theoretical definitions. Such a restrictive view is particularly strong in the United States, where musical competence is in greater demand than universal culture for university teaching positions, whose incumbents must spend much of their time teaching laymen, musicians, and teachers. A survey of musical scholarship in the United States up to 1961 showed a decided preference for problems that were amenable to humanistic methods as against those subject to scientific examination. In this context the following was found a workable definition: "The musicologist is concerned with music that exists, whether as an oral or a written tradition, and with everything that can shed light on its human context."[2] This places the art of music, the works created, performed, and contemplated by men, in the center. The musical work is the principal datum, on which structural analysis, historical explanation, and critical evaluation converge.

A number of European scholars have voiced dissatisfaction with this parochialism. Jacques Handschin has urged that musicology should focus its concern not so much on music as on musical man:

> What, then, is the true object of musicology? It is nothing but man, who, standing in a certain location in space and time, impresses his artistic

[2] Palisca, "American Scholarship in Western Music," in Frank L. Harrison, Mantle Hood, and Claude Palisca, *Musicology* (Englewood Cliffs, 1963; Westport, Connecticut, 1976), p. 116.

striving in an appropriate music; thus man in his musical activity, man artistically forming something that he leaves behind to posterity.[3]

François Lesure, taking up this line of thought, would have musicology ally itself with the "human sciences," which in their methodological innovations have left it far behind. He warns us to beware of isolating works of art from their contexts and the conditions which brought them into being, and particularly from the social, political, and economic functions in which much musical life is embedded.[4]

The opinions just cited are those of historical musicologists who specialize in western music. A similar cleavage between those who would place the emphasis on music and those who would center studies in man and society has developed among those musicologists who specialize in non-western art music and the folk and popular musics of the world.[5] Mieczyslaw Kolinsky[6] has suggested that ethnomusicology contains two distinct types of investigation: comparative musicology and musical anthropology. Here the German musicological tradition clashes with the American anthropological orientation. Kolinsky, who specializes in structural, melodic, rhythmic, and scale analysis, is a product of the school of the psychologist Eric M. von Hornbostel in

---

[3]"Was ist dann aber das wirkliche Objekt der Musikwissenschaft? Es ist nichts anderes als der Mensch, der, an einer gestimmten Stelle des Raumes und der Zeit stehend, sein künstlerisches Sterben in einer ihm gemässen Musik auspräght, also der Mensch in seiner musikalischen Betätigung, der künstlerisch gestaltende Mensch, der der Nachwelt die Erzeugnisse seiner Gestaltung hinterlässt." Jacques Handschin, "Der Arbeitsbereich der Musikwissenschaft," in *Gedenkschrift J. Handschin* (Bern/Stuttgart, 1957), p. 14.

[4]François Lesure, article "Musicologie," in *Encyclopédie de la musique,* ed. François Michel (1961), vol. III; and "The Employment of Sociological Methods in Musical History ("pour une sociologie historique des faits musicaux"), in *International Musicological Society: Report of the Eighth Congress, New York 1961,* ed. Jan LaRue, vol. I (Kassel, 1961), pp. 333-46.

[5]The "special contribution" by Trân van Khê, "Les tendances actuelles de l'ethnomusicologie," provided both general enlightenment and particular facts for my survey. No summary could do justice to the richness of thought and information in this paper, so I have not attempted one. It is good that it can be read in its integral form (in French) in the *Journal of World History* (1970).

[6]Mieczyslaw Kolinsky, "Recent Trends in Ethnomusicology," *Ethnomusicology* 11 (1967), 1-24.

Berlin, which relied greatly on laboratory analysis of music recorded by others in the field. American ethnomusicologists have been typically field workers trained by anthropologists to study music within the context of a whole culture. But even within the company of field workers there is a significant divergence of approach.[7] Some, like Alan P. Merriam, a specialist in African music, study music and behavior in relation to music as detached observers, whereas others, like Mantle Hood, a specialist in Indonesian music, or William P. Malm, in Japanese music, have undergone rigorous apprenticeships as performers with native master musicians and study the music from within the musical culture. Although all of these men profess an interest in both music and behavior as organically wedded, the anthropologist-musicologist tends to concentrate on the behavior of musicians and the function of their music, whereas the musician-ethnologist tends to study the character of musical art as a living component of a culture, developing a sensitivity to its values by immersing himself in its musical idiom.

There is no sign that these streams are merging into a common methodology. Rather, one might say, the eclecticism and diversity of ethnomusicological method today are the surest signs of the vitality of the field.

If the division of musicology into western historical musicology on the one hand and ethnic, non-western, and folk music study on the other must be acknowledged a *fait accompli*, theorists of both disciplines have insistently expressed dissatisfaction with this condition. Historical musicologists have been particularly reproached for failing to take advantage of ethnomusicological methods and insights. Handschin complained that it is "strange that after the appearance of musical psychology and ethnology the historical branch of musicology has continued on its merry way as if nothing had happened."[8]

[7]For the point of view of anthropologists, see, in the UNESCO study, subsection 7, "Music," in Section C ("The Main Fields of Study") of the chapter on *Social and Cultural Anthropology* by Maurice Freedman, pp. 59-62.

[8]". . . curieux que, après l'avènement de la psychologie et de l'ethnologie musicales, la branche historique de la musicologie ait d'abord continué sa marche, comme si rien ne s'était passé." Handschin, "Musicologie et musique," p. 14 in *Internationale Gesellschaft für Musikwissenschaft: Kongress Bericht, Basel, 1949* (Basel, 1949), p. 10.

Charles Seeger has been the most eloquent pleader for a unified musicology and for the application of systematic methods developed in the study of non-western music to contemporary music of the West, not only art music but the total musical scene in all levels of the culture.

> The sooner Western music-historians take off their blinders of Europophilism—as practically all other Western historians have done—and go to work upon the history of non-western musics (and their own popular and folk musics, which are now ethnomusicological data) and ethnomusicologists (hopefully, anthropological as well as musicological, and some of them non-Westerners) summon the courage to go to work upon the ethnomusicology of the music of the West, dealing with it as a whole—its professional as well as its popular and folk idioms—the better it will be for all concerned.[9]

The shrinking interest among today's ethnomusicologists in "universals" about music, such as were sought earlier by comparative musicologists, is paralleled by a decline in generalization among historical musicologists. Werner Korte[10] has attributed this to the disillusionment with the products of the generalization of musical *Geisteswissenschaftler* who tried to carry out Willibald Gurlitt's aim of a synthetic *Stilgeschichtsschreibung.* As expounded in 1918, this synthesis united two directions: 1) *Ausdrucksgeschichte,* the intellectual history behind music, the interpretation of its content, and the clarification of cultural concepts; and 2) *Problemgeschichte,* the study of formal, artistic, and stylistic concepts. It led not to the synthesis Gurlitt envisioned but to unrestrained subjective reaction, the construction of broad artistic style-types like *Gesamtgotik,* a *Formenlehre* of stereotyped categories, and a general dilution of methodological rigor. Korte believes that this method reached a crisis in the 1930-1950 period, and the reaction to it produced a resurgence of the fact-oriented research that Gurlitt tried to replace. There resulted the present trend toward formal technical analysis on the one hand and philological, document-

---

[9]Charles Seeger, Foreword, p. xii in *Studies in Musicology,* ed. James Pruett (Chapel Hill, 1969).
[10]Werner F. Korte, "Struktur und Modell als Information in der Musikwissenschaft," *Archiv für Musikwissenschaft* 21 (1964), 1-22.

oriented research on the other. Friedrich Blume[11] has called the
movement toward documentary and archival study Neo-positivism and
has blamed it for the present isolation of scholars by specialization and
location, the decline of international cooperation, and the alienation of
lay music-lovers and general historians.

The way out of this impasse is seen by many today in a return to the
individual work of art as the starting point of research and explanation.
"The beginning and end of musicological studies lie in sympathetic and
critical examination and evaluation of the individual work of art,"
Lowinsky has said.[12]

What the nature of explanation should be has been the subject of
some discussion recently. Joseph Kerman has suggested that the
ultimate function of musicology is criticism. He sees criticism as the top
rung of a ladder to which the component disciplines of musicology lead.

> Each of the things we [musicologists] do—paleography, transcription,
> repertory studies, archival work, biography, bibliography, sociology,
> *Aufführungspraxis*, schools and influences, theory, style analysis,
> individual analysis—each of these things, which some scholar treats as an
> end in itself, is treated as a step on a ladder.[13]

A work is not understood in isolation but in context. Lowinsky has
challenged Kerman's hierarchical view as debasing certain legitimate
musicological tasks, such as archival studies or transcription, which
may, for some scholars, be ends in themselves. While concurring with
Kerman that scholars should be critics, he would not have criticism ever
part ways from style analysis.

> For if stylistic analysis is understood as the attempt to define a
> composition by describing the modes of behavior of its musical
> components, if criticism is understood to be the discernment and

[11]Friedrich Blume, "Historische Musikforschung in der Gegenwart," *Acta musicologica*
40 (1968), 8-21.
[12]Edward E. Lowinsky, *Tonality and Atonality in Sixteenth-Century Music* (Berkeley
and Los Angeles, 1961), p. 72.
[13]Joseph Kerman, "A Profile for American Musicology," pp. 62-63 in *Journal of the
American Musicological Society* 18 (1965), 61-69.

evaluation of the distinctive, individual traits of that composition, then the more the two are separated, the worse it will be for either.[14]

Along with the tendencies deplored by Blume and Korte must be counted the blind pursuit of the banner of style criticism. Manfred Bukofzer had said: "Style criticism must be recognized as the core of modern musicology. . . . The description of the origin and development of style, their interaction, their transfer from one medium to another, is the central task of musicology."[15] Whereas Bukofzer conceived of style contextually as related to the world of ideas and he subordinated description to understanding, those who followed the slogan of style criticism sacrificed both context and ideas for descriptive, often statistical statements of what occurs in the music of certain composers, genres, or periods. Excessive application of statistical analysis has been criticized as misplaced scientism by Paul Henry Lang: "To impose abstraction upon experience is to fail as a creative scholar while doing badly the work of science. . . ."[16]

Objective description has often been strangely mated with subjective interpretation. Historians who would disclaim allegiance to evolutionary theories of musical development allow evolutionary habits of thought to invade their writing, as Leo Treitler has shown. He finds the growth image constantly evoked by such phrases as "points to the future," "he was a pioneer with respect to . . .", "shows greater mastery of"; or styles are described as "nascent" and "ripe" or "a mixture that rarely resulted in a satisfying synthesis."[17] Musicologists, Treitler observes, treat works as examples of "a collective, impersonal enterprise . . . as manifestations of an Idea, like the shadows in Plato's cave, whose value is measured by the closeness with which they approximate their model, and whose necessities are imposed from without."[18]

[14]Lowinsky, "Character and Purposes of American Musicology; a Reply to Joseph Kerman," p. 224 in *Journal of the American Musicolgical Society* 18 (1965), 222-34.
[15]Manfred Bukofzer, *The Place of Musicology in American Institutions of Higher Learning* (New York, 1957; reprt. New York, 1977), pp. 21, 31.
[16]Paul H. Lang, Editorial, *Musical Quarterly* 50 (1964), p. 219.
[17]Leo Treitler, "On Historical Criticism," *Musical Quarterly* 53 (1967), 203-05.
[18]Ibid., p. 205.

An effective palliative to the tendency to create universals and evolutionary schemes is a concentration upon the individual work. Multidimensional examination of individual artworks could lead not only to better understanding of them but also to more solid grounds for generalization. Treitler[19] has called for "musical analysis in historical context." He views the process as containing a number of overlapping approaches: 1) a search for the significant form of a work, 2) a search for values and schemata that condition apprehension of the work, 3) explanation, particularly causal, of the work in terms of past and contemporary practices and events outside the work, 4) investigation of the music's functions and environmental relations.

The insistence upon historical context in analysis reflects a split that has developed between historians and theorists. Music theory and analysis are taught in conservatories throughout the world mainly by composers. In some countries, particularly England and the United States, this near monopoly extends to universities. Germany, however, is rather exceptional in confiding theory teaching in the universities mainly to musicologists. Nevertheless it is safe to say that the major contributions to music theory in the twentieth century have been made by persons not trained as musicologists and who did or do not consider themselves such. Among these are Heinrich Schenker, Georg Capellen, Bernhard Ziehn, Arnold Schoenberg, Paul Hindemith, Milton Babbitt, and Allen Forte. On the other hand, several prominent music theorists, particularly among those educated in Germany, were musicologically trained, for example Ernst Kurth, Alfred Lorenz, and Felix Salzer. As long as a theorist limits himself to explaining the music he knows exhaustively, as Schenker and Lorenz did, or contemporary music, as with Babbitt, the problem of historical context is not raised. But when theorists apply categories tested and found valid in one repertory to music distant in time from it, they often introduce concepts and explanations quite alien to the mode of thinking of the composers being analyzed.

Less affected by the problem of historical context are analysis, theory, and criticism of contemporary music. Whereas in literary

---

[19]Treitler, "Musical Analysis in an Historical Context," *College Music Symposium* 6 (1966), 75-88.

criticism many of the same writers who comment upon older literature also review and interpret the modern, in music the commentators on older and recent compositions tend to be different sets of persons. Writers on contemporary music are most often composers, performers, or professional critics. Much of their writing has either an ideological or polemic purpose. There abound statements that are mystic, pseudo-philosophical, pseudo-mathematical, and pseudo-scientific.

However, a school of theorists has grown up which aspires to the rigor of mathematics and science.[20] Milton Babbitt, who is the acknowledged leader of the school, has brushed aside distinctions between sciences and humanities and insists "there is but one kind of language, one kind of method for the verbal formulation of 'concepts' and the verbal analysis of such formulations: 'scientific' language and 'scientific' method . . .," and adds that "statements about music must conform to those verbal and methodological requirements which attend the possibility of meaningful discourse in any domain."[21] A theory, if it is truly one, should be "statable as a connected set of axioms, definitions, and theorems, the proofs of which are derived by means of an appropriate logic." None of the theories of the past satisfies these conditions. They have failed by not stating their "empirical domain," and not choosing their "primitives." Another fault has been the futile concern with justifying a theory by ultimate causes, like numerology or nature, outside the formal system of the theory. Babbitt himself has developed a formal theory for the well defined sphere of twelve-tone music.[22] The basic assumptions of the theory are the human ear's consistency in perceiving pitches an octave apart as belonging to the same class, therefore the term "pitch-class," and in perceiving intervals

[20]I acknowledge with thanks the generosity of Allen Forte, who allowed me to study the article, "Musical Theory in the 20th Century, a Survey," prepared for the *Dictionary of 20th-Century Music*, ed. John Vinton (New York, 1974), then in preparation. It illuminated my way through the extensive recent literature on music theory and pointed out for me the significance of many recent developments.
[21]Milton Babbitt, "Past and Present Concepts of the Limits of Music," in *Report of the Eighth Congress*, vol. I (1961), pp. 398-403.
[22]Babbitt, "Some Aspects of Twelve-Tone Composition," *The Score* 12 (1955), 53-61; "Twelve-Tone Invariants as Compositional Determinants," in *Problems of Modern Music*, ed. Paul H. Lang (New York, 1960), pp. 108-21; "Set Structure as a Compositional Determinant," *Journal of Music Theory* 5 (1961), 72-94.

of the same size as identical regardless of pitch, hence the term "interval class." From these characteristics he draws a number of consequences by means of theorems of finite group theory. These theorems deal particularly with variance and invariance, which are applied to forms of the twelve-tone set. Babbitt's theory has been extended by a number of other investigators, including David Lewin, Donald Martino, John Rothgeb, Stefan Bauer-Mengelberg, and Melvin Ferentz. Influenced by Babbitt's method is Forte's theory of set-complexes[23] which is a systematic way to analyze the basic material of pre-twelve-tone music written outside the system of the major and minor scales. Forte's set-complexes are unordered collections of pitches (disregarding octave duplications) having certain arrangements of intervals. His theory permits the analysis of music based on other configurations of notes than the major and minor scale and on other chords than those based on superposition of thirds.

Another mathematical model tending toward a demonstrable music theory is that of information or communication theory. This provides a method of calculating the variety (information) and sameness (redundancy) residing in a composition with respect to a certain characteristic. Investigations have been made, for example, of the comparative rate of information in stable and unstable sections of various compositions[24] measured in terms of the occurrence of twelve pitch classes, and the probability of consecutive intervals.[25] These studies have been on an elementary level not involving dependent probabilities. Despite the huge amount of calculation needed, comparing certain probabilities of a more sophisticated order in different styles may reveal aspects of classical music that otherwise would remain undetected. Information theory has even greater relevance for some forms of contemporary music. Electronic music, for example, has so extended the range of sounds in terms of pitch,

[23]Forte, "A Theory of Set-Complexes for Music," *Journal of Music Theory* 12 (1968), 240-63; "The Domain and Relation of Set-Complex Theory," *Journal of Music Theory* 9 (1965), 173-80.
[24]Lejaren Hiller and Calvert Bean, "Information Theory Analyses of Four Sonata Expositions, *Journal of Music Theory* 10 (1966), 96-137.
[25]See Fritz Winckel, "Musik—VI. Informationstheorie, in *Die Musik in Geschichte und Gegenwart* IV (1955), 967-70.

dynamics, divisibility in time, and so on, that both the limits of the channels of communication such as phonograph records, and of the human receptor need to be studied. Iannis Xenakis[26] has shown that what he calls "stochastic" music can be composed at various levels of determinacy in which general and transition probabilities are regulated according to the desired outcome, aesthetic aim, or other function. Aleatoric or chance music and that which relies partly on improvisation is probably more susceptible to study in terms of information theory than to more conventional theories. Abraham Moles[27] has also suggested the relevance of information theory to the understanding of the dynamics and effects of mixed media, such as dance or operatic recitative.

The limits of perception and apprehension—and therefore of communication—so far as certain kinds of contemporary music are concerned have been studied by Robert Francès and Albert Wellek. Francès[28] asked a group of composers, conductors, and analysts to distinguish between fragments based on two different twelve-tone sets and found their identifications erred in more than 50% of the cases. This casts some doubt, Francès remarks, on the unifying efficacy of a twelve-tone series. Wellek[29] introduced errors of performance or intonation in a piece of Schoenberg and found that music students could spot only a third or a fourth of the alterations in this music, whereas they almost never failed to pick out such errors in pieces of Dussek or C. P. E. Bach.

A number of recent analytical studies of music have required a vast amount of data that could not have been handled without a computer. However, artificial languages for encoding music and programs for

---

[26]Iannis Xenakis, *Musiques formelles* (Paris, 1963).
[27]Abraham Moles, *Théorie de l'information et perception esthétique* (Paris, 1958) (English edn., *Information Theory and Aesthetic Perception*, 1966); see also, by Moles, the sub-section "The Informational Approach" in the chapter of the UNESCO study preceding this essay.
[28]Robert Francès, *La Perception de la musique* (Paris, 1958); see also, by Francès, the sub-section "The Experimental Approach," in the chapter of the UNESCO study preceding this essay.
[29]Albert Wellek, "Expériences comparées sur la perception de la musique dodécaphonique," *Sciences de l'art* 3 (1966); see also, by Wellek, in the chapter of the UNESCO study preceding this essay, the sub-section "The Pyschological Approach," paragraph I: "The Pyschology of Music Hearing."

analyzing it had first to be devised by the authors of these studies. Bauer-Mengelberg has invented a comprehensive music encoding language called the Ford-Columbia language after his sponsors. Forte[30] worked out a program for the analytic reading of music scores in a language, SNOBOL 3, for which he wrote a manual.[31]

Although historians of music have been slow in exploiting the computer, a few recent projects are paving the way for others by coming to terms with some of the problems of encoding older notations. Raymond Erickson[32] has modified the Ford-Columbia language to accommodate the notation of twelfth-century Notre Dame polyphony for a study of rhythmic problems and melodic structure in *organum purum*. Murray Gould[33] has published a scheme for translating the plain chant notation of the *Liber usualis* into symbols available on a key-punch machine. Nanna Schiødt and Bjarner Svejgaard[34] have devised a scheme for analyzing the operation of melodic formulae in the Byzantine Sticherarion. As programming and encoding languages become standardized, as "software" is developed for program conversion to many forms of computer input, many scholars now intimidated by the technical problems will be attracted to high-speed data processing for analysis.

A much more common use of computers in musicology has been for indexing and bibliographical purposes. Indexing of purely verbal material, such as titles, has profited by the advancement of information retrieval generally. The most notable project is the *Répertoire Internationale de la Littérature Musicale* (*RILM*), headed by Barry S. Brook and established in 1966 by the International Musicological

[30]Forte, "A Program for the Analytic Reading of Scores," *Journal of Music Theory* 8 (1964), 136-83.
[31]Forte, *SNOBOL Primer* (Cambridge, 1967).
[32]Raymond Erickson, "Musical Analysis and the Computer," *Journal of Music Theory* 9 (1965), 173-80.
[33]Murray Gould, "A Keypunchable Notation for the *Liber usualis*", in *Elektronische Datenverarbeitung in der Musikwissenschaft*, ed. Harald Heckmann (Regensburg, 1967), pp. 25-40.
[34]Hanna Schiødt and Bjarner Svejgaard, "Application of Computer Techniques to the Analysis of Byzantine Sticherarion-Melodies," in Heckmann, *Elektronische Datenverarbeitung*, pp. 187-201.

Society and the International Association of Music Libraries under the sponsorship of the American Council of Learned Societies. *RILM* has indexed in some depth all the significant literature on music that has appeared since January 1, 1967, and is intended to provide a model for indexing in other fields.

As opposed to bibliography, indexing of music is more problematic because of the encoding problem. Some of the indexing projects now in progress are those of Jan LaRue on themes of eighteenth-century symphonies[35] and Harry Lincoln[36] of sixteenth-century frottola melodies. Similar thematic indices in such fields as troubadour melodies, tropes and sequences, motets, masses, chansons, and madrigals, not to mention sonatas and concertos, have either been contemplated or begun, and when completed could be a boon to the many musicologists constantly seeking to identify composers, authenticate works, describe variants, and search for sources.

Ethnomusicologists have made comparatively little use of the computer. This is understandable, since much of the data concerning a culture and its music must be expressed in narrative statements. On the other hand, in comparing melodies of one culture to another or of neighboring peoples, such as related tribes, or in generalizing upon the style of one culture, computational methods would be as useful as they are in the study of historical repertories. The actual tendency has been, rather, the development of various melody-writing instruments, such as Seeger's melograph[37] and Uppsala University's "Mona,"[38] which permit monophonic performance to be represented and visually analyzed in every detail.

The "information explosion" is both a blessing and a cause for concern. When information is so easily gathered, stored, and analyzed,

[35]Jan LaRue and Marian W. Cobin, "The Ruge-Seignolay Catalogue: An Exercise in Automated Entries," in Heckmann, *Elektronische Datenverarbeitung*, pp. 41-56.
[36]Harry Lincoln, "Some Criteria and Techniques for Developing Computerized Thematic Indices," in Heckmann, *Elektronische Datenverarbeitung*, pp. 57-62.
[37]Charles Seeger, "Versions and Variants of the Tunes of 'Barbara Allen'," in Institute of Ethnomusicology, University of California, Los Angeles, *Reports* 2 (1966), 120-67.
[38]Ingmar Bengtsson, "On Melody Registration and 'Mona'," in Heckmann, *Elektronische Datenverarbeitung*, pp. 136-74.

we can be deluged with data. The scholar will need to know when to stop, to recognize the point of diminishing relevance.

Arthur Mendel in the first public address to the New York Congress of the International Musicological Society in 1961 asked why we inquire into the history of music. It is suggested, he said, that we do so to learn from the past how to act in the future. He rejected this utilitarian explanation as not consistent with practice, since very few readers of history deal with the future; for example, composers make little use of our knowledge of the music of the remote past. Mendel concluded that we study history of music primarily "because we have a passion for understanding things, for being puzzled and solving our puzzles; because we are curious and will not be satisfied until our curiosity rests."[39]

This answer will not satisfy everyone, since it could be objected that there are too many things to understand, too many puzzles to solve. There are obviously priorities. Solution of problems in which others besides musicologists have a stake have such priority.

Musicology must continue to benefit performers and conductors and through them their public. The rediscovery of Bach in the early nineteenth century and since then of hundreds of other composers both earlier and later has revolutionized the repertory of concert and recorded music. It has also created problems for performers who must relive a practice buried in the past. At first it seemed that having critical editions that present the music in the state in which it left the composer's pen would provide the basis for the restoration of the authentic sound of the music. By now such editions are common, but it has become evident in the meantime that composers before the nineteenth century, at least, left much to the taste and elaboration of the player.[40] Concerning the interpretation of the composer's text, simple answers once accepted have given way to multiple answers, as instruction books and other literary and musical documents have been read more carefully and exhaustively. It is obvious that most of the issues cannot be settled

[39]Arthur Mendel, "Evidence and Explanation," p. 4 in *Report of the Eighth Congress*, vol. II (1962), pp. 3-18.
[40]See Mendel, "The Service of Musicology to the Practical Musician," in *Some Aspects of Musicology* (New York, 1957, reprt. New York, 1977).

definitively and that several alternate solutions may be equally authentic. To pass on to the performer these options in such a way that he can understand them and use them artfully remains a challenge to musicology.[41]

Another obvious priority is to make available to the musical public the means of understanding significant music of all traditions and cultures.

Being a relatively young field of university study, music has had to guard jealously its identity as a scholarly discipline; so in most countries it has failed to establish close ties with the public or lower levels of education. The music scholar tends to operate in the hermetic atmosphere of libraries, institutes, and seminars and to communicate through specialized reviews. Few of his discoveries and interpretations leak out to the general public. In earlier days, when the scholarly readership was small, musicologists were compelled to appeal to the amateur if they were to see their work in print. But today only a small proportion of active scholars write books of general interest. On the other hand, other channels have opened up, such as radio-television networks, most notably those in Germany, England, Italy, and France, which have confided the direction of important series of programs to scholars. Also a number of periodicals such as *The Musical Times* (London), the *Saturday Review* (New York), the *Oesterreichische Musikzeitschrift* (Vienna) carry articles of scholarly depth for the amateur and musician.

There are also encouraging signs that university scholars are establishing contacts with elementary and secondary schools. In England and Germany, where the prospective secondary school teacher is not isolated from the normal music program of the university, he is frequently exposed to the point of view of the scholar in his training. In the United States, on the other hand, elementary and secondary school teachers are trained mainly in university schools of education and have relatively little contact with musical scholarship. Recently, however, several projects sponsored by the federal government and private

---

[41]See Luigi Ferdinando Tagliavini, "Prassi esecutiva e metodo musicologico," in *Internationale Gesellschaft für Muskwissenschaft: Kongress Bericht, Salzburg 1964* (Kassel, 1964), I, 19-24.

foundations in the United States have brought scholars, composers, theorists, teachers, and professors of education together.[42] In Italy a recent legislative proposal (Chamber of Deputies, no. 4327, 27 July 1967)[43] projects a reorganization of musical studies in which holders of degrees in musicology would teach history of music in the *scuole secondarie superiori* and in the conservatories, as well as in the universities.

Through rapports such as these with the general education of young persons and with the public, musicologists will discover yardsticks of relevance that can restore a balance between fact-finding for its own sake and the needs of the world of music and society at large. Friedrich Blume, editor of the great fourteen-volume encyclopedia *Die Musik in Geschichte und Gegenwart,* addressed principally to professional scholars and musicians, has clearly expressed the music historian's concern with this larger responsibility, and what he says applies equally well to theory and ethnomusicology:

> The hunger for musical understanding cannot be satisfied with recipes for alchemists' clandestine cookery. . . . Music is a cultural resource of mankind and not a handtool for the musician. Interest in the history of music does not restrict itself to the narrow circle of historians. We should remain concerned that music history not lose its place in the general education of the *homines bonae voluntatis,* that it not trickle away into the dry streams of narrow professionalism.[44]

---

[42]See *Current Musicology* 2 (1966), 129-72, a special section: "Musicology and Music Education;" see also *College Music Symposium* 9 (1969), 36-47 and 65-111.

[43]See Andrea Mascagni, "L'insegnamento della musica in Italia," *Nuova rivista musicale italiana* 3 (1969), 55-78.

[44]"Der Hunger nach dem Verstehen von Musik kann nicht mit den Rezepten alchimistischer Geheimküchen gestillt werden. . . . Musik ist ein Kulturgut der Menschheit und nicht ein Handwerkzeug für den Musiker. Das Interesse für die Geschichte der Musik beschränkt sich nicht auf den engen Kreis von Historikern. Wir sollten bemüht bleiben, dass Musikgeschichte im universalen Bildungsbedürfnis der *homines bonae voluntatis* ihren Platz nicht verliert, dass sie nicht auf den Durststrecken engen Fachdenkens dahinwelkt." Blume, "Historische Musikforschung in der Gegenwart," pp. 15 and 21.

Archival Research

Jeremy Noble

Just over a hundred years ago the British Army suffered one of its
bloodier defeats at a place called Isandhlwana, in what was then
Zululand. The commander-in-chief, Lord Chelmsford, convinced that
the main body of the Zulu forces was due north of his position, marched
off with half his army to meet them. No sooner was he safely out of the
way than the Zulus came round the other side of the hill in vastly
superior numbers and massacred the force Chelmsford had left behind.

Jeremy Noble, Associate Professor of Music, State University of New York at Buffalo,
knows his way around the archives as well as anyone, as demonstrated by his remarkable
report concerning Josquin des Prez ("New Light on Josquin's Benefices," in *Josquin des
Prez*, ed. Edward E. Lowinsky with the collaboration of Bonnie J. Blackburn [London,
1976], pp. 76-102). He is in a good position to take a critical view of what his colleagues
have done with the spoils.

I was reminded of this unfortunate event not long after I had accepted Professor Palisca's kind invitation to speak about archival research in today's panel on methodologies.

It had seemed to me at first that the only likely objection to archival studies would come from what one might call the analytical absolutists, that is to say the small (I hope small) number of musicologists who would reject entirely the historical component of our craft in favor of an exclusive concentration on its primary object: the individual musical work. But when I said as much to a colleague who has spent far more of his life looking at archives than I have, his reaction was quite different. Archival research, he felt, needed to be protected not from its avowed enemies so much as from its professed friends—not from the anti-historians, but from the incompetent historians, the unimaginative scholars and would-be scholars who are urged by their advisers and by fashion into a study from which they can derive little enlightenment and which they may be tempted to use as the basis for a specious authority and the propagation of pseudo-historical errors. Faced with this double threat, I feel constrained to avoid Lord Chelmsford's error of judgment (to give it no harsher name), and instead to hunker down in my own, very modest, position and defend it as best I can against all attacks—from whichever side of the hill they may come.

And it really is quite a modest position, I think. For a start, I would certainly not want to maintain that all aspirant musicologists should be trained to do archival work, even if this were possible, given the diversity of demands that archival research can make on us. It is clearly more important that students be given a sound grammatical and syntactical understanding of at least those musical styles that are central to their own tradition: music itself is the midpoint of our study; social context, biography, only secondary. On the other hand, I do believe that all those who are going to make use of biographical or historical information, even if it is only to the extent of paraphrasing an entry in *Grove* in order to face the next morning's class, should be encouraged to understand and appreciate the kind of interpretative work that underpins their own rather too easy assumption of omniscience, and not to take it for granted as a kind of anonymous service which need be neither acknowledged nor critically examined. Too many musicologists have tended to behave like old-fashioned *patresfamilias,* content to leave so humble an activity as the provision of meals to servants or wives. But just as liberated husbands have found their way into the kitchen, and in so doing have acquired a critical awareness of the food they have, after all, got to eat, so more musicologists seem to be getting into the archival kitchen these days, and on the whole benefiting from it by acquiring an increased awareness of the historical context of their work. I believe, in fact, that anyone who is engaged in historical research should be encouraged (not forced) to seek out its archival dimensions, and not to rest until he has satisfied himself either that there are no relevant ones or that he has explored them to the full extent of their usefulness.

That usefulness, I would be the first to admit, is in the nature of the case limited. Archives, after all, are the repository of only one (albeit quite an important one) of the sub-sections of history's raw materials, in particular the official lives of institutions and of the individuals who have worked for them. We all—at least those of us who are old enough to pay taxes—know how important it is to have our own little archives. In addition to the accounts of our financial income and expenditures they will probably also contain documents that have a bearing on our' legal status, such things as birth certificates and passports, for instance; perhaps leases and contracts, as well as (on a more personal level) old diaries and correspondence. We amass all this material for our own use, of course, and it is quite unlikely that it will be of much interest to anyone else. But if by any chance someone were misguided enough to want to write our biography, how glad they would be that we had kept it! It might not tell them much about our character or achievements (if any), but it would at least help them to avoid egregious errors of time and place, and to get the historical groundwork accurately in position.

Now archives of the kind we have in mind today provide exactly the same kind of information, and with exactly the same kind of limitations, for *institutions,* whether extant or defunct. If they are defunct (like the French monarchy, for example), whatever is left of their archives will probably have fetched up in national or regional collections, and it will be no small part of our task to track them down even before we can sift through them. If the institutions are still extant, like the Roman Catholic Church, for instance, or the Paris Opéra (I don't mean to suggest any equivalence), their archives will probably still be at least partly in their own possession, which can give rise to problems of a different order. In either case, though, it would seem to me absurd for musicologists, insofar as they consider themselves to be historians at all, to neglect the information that can be gleaned from these collections, given time, patience, and the kind of skills that can only be acquired in doing the job.

And in fact it seems to me that such collections have been increasingly utilized by musicologists in the last two or three decades. Not that they had been allowed merely to gather dust before then. Particularly in countries which were striving for a sense of national identity, local patriotism gave rise to a great deal of research in the nineteenth century; one thinks of vander Straeten in Belgium, of Caffi, Davari, Bertolotti, Cittadella, Motta, and many others in Italy.[1] And even if one is tempted to regard some of their work as too unsystematic to be more than mere antiquarianism, one can also point to examples of research carried out with real historical sophistication. To name just one, Charles Sanford Terry's biography of Bach, first published in 1928, was exemplary in its handling of documentary evidence, no doubt because Terry himself was a trained historian.[2]

But there can be no doubt, I think, that archival research has become a growth industry in the last twenty years or so, as a comparison between *Grove V* and *The New Grove* will very quickly demonstrate. Particularly if we look at the entries on fifteenth- and sixteenth-century

[1]Edmond vander Straeten, *La Musique aux Pays-bas avant le XIXe siècle* (Brussels, 1867-88; reprt. New York, 1969, with an introduction by Edward E. Lowinsky). Francesco Caffi, *Storia della musica sacra nella già Cappella Ducale di San Marco in Venezia dal 1318 al 1797* (Venice, 1854; reprt. Bologna, 1973). Stefano Davari, "La musica a Mantova . .", *Rivista storica mantovana* I (1884), 53-71; reprt. Mantua, 1975. Antonio Bertolotti, *Musici alla Cortedei Gonzaga in Mantova dal secolo VI and XVIII* (Milan, 1980; reprt. Geneva, 1978). Luigi Napoleone Cittadella, *Notizie relative a Ferrara* (Ferrara, 1864-68). Emilio Motta, "Musici alla Corte degli Sforza," *Archivio storico lombarda* 14 (1887), 29-64, 278-340, 514-61; reprt. separately, Geneva, 1977.
[2]Charles Sanford Terry, *Bach, a Biography* (London, 1928; 2nd rev. edn., 1933).

composers we can see how a wider and more comprehensive use of archival material is gradually bringing our picture of the music of that period into clearer focus. Craig Wright's research on Dufay, Herbert Kellman's on Josquin, Horst Leuchtmann's on Lassus, Lewis Lockwood's on Willaert—to mention only a few conspicuous examples—have given us an altogether clearer idea of those major figures and their creative development.[3] But it is not only the peaks that are standing forth more clearly: the mist is rolling back from the foothills, too, and it is becoming possible to place even minor figures in something like their correct historical perspective. Nor is this true only of the Renaissance. Admittedly the archival material gets rapidly thinner as one pushes back before the fifteenth century, but for the host of operatic and instrumental composers of the seventeenth century the situation has improved almost as dramatically as for those of the Renaissance. I would be the first to admit that all this new information does not necessarily help us in coming to grips with individual works: if that were so, we should expect those scholars with the greatest archival experience to show the greatest interest in, and sensitivity to, nuances of style, and that is not always the case. But neither is it necessarily *not* the case. There is nothing in archival research that automatically blasts the musical tastebuds, and any evidence that helps us to make the relevant comparisons, to look for plausible lines of influence instead of chronologically or geographically improbable ones, is surely to be welcomed.

At the same time I want to enter a caveat that may perhaps arouse some resistance. I said earlier that archives provide us with the raw material for the lives of institutions, and grateful as I am for all the new details that are emerging about individual composers, I have become convinced that that is not the most fruitful or important use to which archives can be put. I used to think it was. In fact I only started visiting archives because I was concerned to check the original readings and contexts of documents that I found quoted in various books (notably

---

[3]Craig Wright, "Dufay at Cambrai: Discoveries and Revisions," *Journal of the American Musicological Society* 28 (1975), 175-229. Horst Leuchtmann, *Orlando di Lasso: sein Leben* (Wiesbaden, 1976).

Osthoff's Josquin monograph)[4] but which seemed to me not fully intelligible as they were presented to us. But the more I delved into the account books and the files of correspondence from which these details had been selected, the more I became convinced that it was not intellectually respectable to emulate little Jack Horner, who (if you remember the nursery rhyme) sat in a corner eating a Christmas pie; he put in his thumb and pulled out a plum, saying "Oh what a good boy am I!" This is what many earlier scholars were content to do, and although some of our own generation have broken through to a wider viewpoint (I think, for example of Frank D'Accone's work in Florence),[5] too many of us still tend to concentrate only on the search for plums, partly out of a desire to spare our readers the boredom of wading through trivia, and partly through a natural preoccupation with big names. Now I would be the last to try to play down the distinction between greatness and mediocrity: on the contrary, I think it needs to be insisted upon in our egalitarian age. But it is only when we have some grasp of such institutions as the Papal Choir, the various royal and ducal chapels, and at a later date the various opera and theatre companies, with their diverse functions, duties, and traditions, that we can fully appreciate the stature and the individuality of the few geniuses who happened to work in or with them. Astronomers don't study comets without studying the more predictable bodies, and for that matter the space itself, through which they erratically pass: nor should we, collectively, confine our attentions exclusively to geniuses.

Ideally, I should like to see on our library shelves a series of institutional studies, a kind of musicological *Guide Bleu* or *Touring Club Italiano*, if you like, in which one could look up the precise context in which whatever composer we happen to be studying worked: who his colleagues were, how he ranked among them in pay or privileges, how their functions were traditionally defined, what musical forces they had at their disposal—and that last item, incidentally, is a whole branch of

[4]Helmuth Osthoff, *Josquin Desprez* (Tutzing, 1962-65).
[5]Notably in "The Musical Chapels at the Florentine Cathedral and Baptistry During the First Half of the 16th Century," *Journal of the American Musicological Society* 25 (1971), 1-50.

archival study in itself, which has already contributed much to our notions of performance-practice, and undoubtedly has still more to contribute in the future. If fellowships grew on trees (and, for that matter, students with the talent and inclination for this kind of work) one might set about organizing such a project, a sort of multi-volume musicological gazetteer. But in practice I think we have to recognize that the day for that kind of project has passed. There is never again likely to be the money or the cheap labor available that made possible such great nineteenth-century historical series as the *Calendar of State Papers,* to take a familiar example. Nor do most scholars, fully involved in the profession of teaching, have the free time to undertake work of that kind and bring it to a conclusion in a single lifetime.

So it seems to me that the kind of computerized central storage-system for archival material (known provisionally as RENARC) upon which some of us have been working under Professor Leeman Perkins's chairmanship may well represent the best possible contemporary solution. All those of us who have worked in archives know what it is to have unused material left in our notebooks—material, that is to say, which has not fitted into the book or article we have published, but which may nevertheless be precisely what someone else is looking for. Rather than let such material disappear into obscurity again—it might be a single payment-entry or perhaps the general description of a whole series of registers—it would seem to me infinitely preferable to put it into a communal "bank," docketed with the name of its original discoverer, of course, who would presumably retain some kind of tenuous rights over it, but not the right to prevent publication. At all events, I think that unless we are going to take the line that archival research is a pure waste of time and a distraction from the musicologist's true function (whatever that may be), it will be necessary to devise some such means both of storing and of disseminating its results.

Applications of the History of Ideas

Maria Rika Maniates

Since my assignment offered an embarrassment of riches, it seemed advisable to focus on two topics, both fairly recent and provocative — namely, symbolism and rhetoric.

It goes without saying that writings about music ought to assume their proper place in intellectual history. To judge from the many fine studies and critical editions that have appeared in recent years, the field shows renewed vigor. Testimony of this was the impressive expertise

Maria Rika Maniates, Professor of Musicology in the Faculty of Music at the University of Toronto, currently Connaught Senior Fellow in the Humanities, drew in many important ways on the history of ideas in her *Mannerism in Italian Music and Cultures, 1530-1630* (Chapel Hill, 1979). While some reviewers have already had their says and others are still pondering it, she takes a critical look at what her colleagues have been doing in applications of the history of thought.

evident in a 1979 AMS panel chaired by Claude Palisca during which scholars described their triumphs, problems, and methods in translating primary theoretical sources. All the same, I believe we must make a more concerted effort to render this expertise intelligible to other humanist scholars, even if this means recasting our vocabulary or reordering our priorities.

Moreover, one cannot ignore the issue of the relevance to music of intellectual history, be the ideas under examination speculative, aesthetic, descriptive, or didactic. Put in a nutshell, the question is: what has the world of verbal discourse to do with the activities of musicians? This question is crucial to symbolic and rhetorical exegeses of music. In view of the debates at our meetings and in our journals, I am sure we are aware that a substantial number of musicologists maintain that history of ideas cannot illuminate in any intrinsic way the workings of compositions or the historicity of musical languages. This conviction about epistemology deserves respect and rebuttal from those holding the opposite view. But in this brief essay, I invite you to explore with me the methods used to validate connections between music and ideas, for some of them generate misgivings among historians who sympathize with the premise that certain practices exhibit symbolic or rhetorical intentions.

One way history of ideas influences our interpretation of such intentions has to do with construing the tacit structure of thought patterns of the past that lie beneath the surface ploys of learned discourse. I mention only three such structures, all of which bear directly on the topics under discussion.[1]

First, the use in the sixteenth century of *analogia* (obvious resemblances) and *signatura* (hidden signs) to identify or to fabricate correspondences among divergent concepts of experiences and objects. The *modus operandi* of this quasi-hermetic procedure gave way in the seventeenth century to explanatory propositions made up of cause and

[1]See Michel Foucault, *The Order of Things: an Archaeology of the Human Sciences* (London, 1970); Frances A. Yates, *Giordano Bruno and the Hermetic Tradition* (London, 1964); James H. Jensen, *The Muses' Concord: Literature, Music and the Visual Arts in the Baroque Age* (Bloomington, 1976); George Kennedy, *Classical Rhetoric and its Christian and Secular Tradition from Ancient to Modern Times* (Chapel Hill, 1980).

effect sequences, a tacit structure based on the new science and its logic. And although we may find the latter to be more akin to modern epistemology, it is fair to say that the flights of fancy endemic to much sixteenth-century thinking all too often dwindled into mechanical constructs of causality. This is especially true for certain problems of musical meaning broached by theorists and philosophers.

Second, the complex matter of the episteme of mind/soul, its appetitive, sensible, and rational levels. This structure pertains to what is now called faculty psychology, and it was transmitted from the ancient Greeks down to the sixteenth century, taking on different hierarchical values along the way and reaching its final formulation in the seventeenth century.

Finally, the gradual move from "primary" to "secondary" rhetoric, a move that reflected the change from the extemporized to the written word. In the case of this third structure, it is difficult, if not impossible, to demarcate any definite stages. All the same, historians of rhetoric recognize that the major shift from improvised oratory to written literature, particularly in printed form, carried with it a fundamental alteration in the functions ascribed to the art of rhetoric. Insofar as this alteration was rarely acknowledged in primary sources, it acted as a tacit structure governing the systems and values imputed to verbal discourse. And more to the point for us, "secondary" rhetoric as it was applied to written communication had a decisive influence on the ways in which music theorists transmogrified rhetoric to suit their purposes.

For the subject of symbolism, I am being a shoemaker in limiting my remarks to Renaissance studies.[2] Art and literature seem to be the most fertile fields, because their modes can portray cognitive ideas in visual and linguistic manners, and scholars have access to primary documents on method. In this context, finding incontrovertible evidence of symbolic intentions and of specific symbols in music is a hazardous enterprise. Perhaps this is one reason why musicologists usually employ conflation, a method of amassing a wide range of disparate evidence based on their sensitivity and breadth of knowledge rather than on firm proof of any direct relation to the music under scrutiny. I hasten to add

[2]Maniates, "Musical Symbolism," *The World of Music* 3 (1978), 38-55.

that this method operates in art and literature as well; for instance, the illustrious tradition founded by Panofsky, a tradition that has produced some brilliant essays on symbols in art. Recently, there has been a decided retrenchment from what is now considered too undisciplined an application of history of ideas, and with it a new emphasis on hard facts to support the actuality and meaning of symbols. And even though the problems for the interpreter of music are different in certain fundamental respects, it seems pertinent to suggest that we should re-examine our premises in musical hermeneutics. Edward A. Lippman's essay offers many valuable pointers on how to go about this task.[3]

Rigorous method can prove frustrating, as I once found out. In the Dijon chansonnier there is an anonymous piece sandwiched between two combinative works by Ockeghem.[4] Each of its two inner parts quotes a Marian chant while the upper part presents a French poem to the Virgin Mary. This poem describes the Lady of the Apocalypse, clothed with the sun, a crown of twelve stars around her head and the moon beneath her feet. Vertically along one margin the scribe has copied the Latin verse from the Bible. I considered the symbolism to be striking, and began looking for precise documentation that might elucidate the piece and the circumstances of its composition. My research netted an assortment of bits and pieces from written and iconographical sources, including several symbolic referents for the Lady and a theological muddle over the legitimacy of the Virgin reading. Interesting as this information was, it did not amount to much. And so I set the project aside for future reconsideration.

I doubt I shall be so fortunate as Charles Warren, who, in his article on Dufay's *Nuper rosarum flores* and Brunelleschi's dome for the cathedral in Florence, argues cogently for a close connection between two media, two artists, and two works indisputably linked by social

---

[3]"The Problem of Musical Hermeneutics: a Protest and Analysis," *Art and Philosophy,* ed. S. Hook (New York, 1966), pp. 307-55.
[4]*Permanent vierge-Pulchra es-Sancta Dei genitrix.* Dijon: Bibliothèque de la Ville, ms 517, fol. 165v-166r.

circumstance.[5] Another splendid set of studies is Edward E. Lowinsky's work on the Fortuna pieces.[6] His material on non-musical depictions of the goddess furnishes general evidence of a symbolic tradition, and this does serve a purpose. But it is the musical context that must justify precise symbolic intent in the pieces themselves, and Lowinsky does not let us down. The two identifiable devices in the repertory exemplify methodological issues. The first one, quoting pre-existent tunes about Fortuna, belongs to an established tradition—namely, the emblematic citation of known melodies whose presence adds an allegorical dimension to the main text. The second, hexachord mutation, is arguable for several reasons. We have not as yet reached unanimity on the textual interpretation of *musica ficta,* and I am not sure we ever will. This disagreement impinges on assessing the sonic quality of mutation, which quality is purportedly symbolic in the works. Conflicting opinions notwithstanding, one is convinced by the suasive power of Lowinsky's thesis—to wit, mutation symbolizes the mutability of Fortuna's wheel. Given the ups and downs of various "fictive" polemics, I suspect the symbolic magic of this device has lost none of its power.

Willem Elders's monograph merits comment because it raises important questions about methodology.[7] Elders concentrates solely on exhaustive coverage of musical sources; this is a commendable, if not always a practicable or successful strategy. His most reliable readings result from fully developed musical contexts: emblematic *cantus firmi, soggetti cavati,* canons, and the like. But what are we to do whenever research turns up one or very few pieces, either because we overlooked other sources or because that is all there is? In a few such cases, his remedy is to link a single external allegory to an isolated musical symbol. These connections remain tenuous in the absence of intellectual history and of proof that the composer or copyist knew the particular allegory in question. Moreover, the examples inserted with feeble and

---

[5]"Brunelleschi's Dome and Dufay's Motet," *Musical Quarterly* 59 (1973), 92-105.
[6]"The Goddess Fortuna in Music," *Musical Quarterly* 29 (1943), 45-77; "Matthaeus Greiter's *Fortuna,*" *Musical Quarterly* 42 (1956), 500-19, and 43 (1957), 68-75.
[7]*Studien zur Symbolik in der musik der alten Niederländer* (Bilthoven, 1968).

non-existent contexts raise some doubt as to the wisdom of pursuing this method exclusively.

It must be said here that some kinds of symbols are more obvious than others and consequently that their contexts lend themselves to discovery. In the best of circumstances, overt symbols are conspicuous whenever they seem not to answer strictly musical requirements (if such a thing can be clearly adjudicated). Circumstances have a way of being anything but the best, and this happens with covert symbols whose interpretation impels us to negotiate the impenetrable underbrush of hermetic lore. By definition, camouflaged symbols operate on two levels: as normal ingredients of design and as carriers of hidden meaning. Musical contexts do not seem to be helpful, unless one is convinced of the utility of quantitative evidence.

Let us suppose, for the sake of argument, that I found a high number of canons for two and for three voices in the motets of one composer and also noticed that half of these texts dealt in each case with with Immaculate Conception and the Holy Trinity. Am I entitled to read each kind of canon as a symbol or emblem of each idea? And may I then go on to say that the remaining canons are identical symbols, bringing a tertiary level of meaning to other texts on different themes? To guard against over-interpretation I could test the coherence of tertiary allegory, and then discard those pieces whose canon seems predominantly structural in nature. This would be fairly easy to do with the Immaculate Conception/canon-for-two-voices set. But according to *doctrina christiana* the Holy Trinity is everywhere, and I wonder if there is a religious text where trinitarian symbolism would be incongruous.

This kind of symbolism becomes even more problematic when we encounter details of a distinctly innocuous cast. In this respect, the current spate of studies on number symbolism is fraught with perils. Considering the cryptic nature of the symbols, one is not surprised to find that the musical contexts erected by such scholars as Henze,

Heikamp, van Crevel, Elders, and Vellekoop are highly hypothetical.[8] The situation is not improved by displays of cabalistic virtuosity or by indiscriminate concatentations of gematria, puns, and cabala. Even if critics were to discount those computations they deem to be fortuitous or fantastic, the remaining instances cannot be so easily dismissed. As things stand, neither can they be so easily accredited as intentional. And to successfully accomplish the latter, recourse to the general currency of *signatura* does not suffice.

   History of ideas is equally pertinent to rhetorical readings.[9] While it is perhaps defensible to use rhetoric in a systematic way, this method can lead to some difficulties if it is not judiciously handled. I remember recently hearing a paper in which rhetorical material was culled haphazardly from ancient writings to prove that avant-garde music of our century is *not* formless. Is there a compelling reason to explicate an articulative device in a Stockhausen piece as a figure from one of Cicero's treatises? Just because words and tones exist in a temporal dimension, it does not follow that rhetoric illuminates all kinds of musical forms. After all, rhetoric is only one tool for describing linguistic structures, and for this reason it is not a suitable substitute for "pattern-communication" through music. A similar confusion is apparent, in my view, in Peter Williams's study, "*Figurenlehre* from Monteverdi to Wagner."[10] For one thing, *Lehre* is immaterial to some

[8] Marianne Henze, *Studien zu den Messenkompositionen Johannes Ockeghem* (Berlin, 1968). Dieter Heikamp, "Zur Struktur der Messe 'L'Homme armé super voces musicales' von Josquin Desprez," *Die Musikforschung* 19 (1966), 121-41. Marius van Crevel, edns. of Obrecht's *Missa Sub tuum praesidium* and *Missa Maria zart* in *Opera Omnia*, vols. 6 and 7 (Amsterdam, 1959 and 1964). Willem Elders, "Das Symbol in der Musik von Josquin des Prez," *Acta musicologica* 41 (1969), 164-85. Kees Vellekoop, "Zusammenhänge zwischem Text und Zahl in der Kompositionsart Jacob Obrechts: Analyse der Motette, 'Parce Domine'," *Tijdschrift van de Vereniging voor Nederlandse Muziekgeschiedenis* 20 (1966), 97-119.

[9] Maniates, "Music and Rhetoric: Faces of Cultural History in the Renaissance and the Baroque," *Israel Studies in Musicology* 3 (1982), in press.

[10] *Musical Times* 120 (1979), 476-79, 571-73, 648-50, 816-18. The italics are mine.

of his musical examples, and for another, all *Figuren* are patterns but not all patterns are *Figuren.*

The juxtaposition of music and rhetoric in writings from the sixteenth to the eighteenth centuries, together with its putative reflection in concurrent practices, warrants serious consideration. And in this area we find many stimulating studies by a group of scholars who have imparted a sense of excitement and adventure to the field. George Buelow's authoritative article in *The New Grove* commands admiration on many counts, not least of which is his tabulation of the tangled web of terminology in the primary sources.[11] Those of us who labor with our notecards owe him a resounding vote of thanks. On a more detailed level, Claude V. Palisca's study of Burmeister exposes the pros and cons of the theorist's analytic method and its outcome with respect to Lasso's motet, *In me transierunt.*[12]

To my mind, there lurk on the peripheries of these studies some unanswered questions. First, why did music theorists refer to rhetoric at all? Second, how does this rhetorical piracy jibe with each system? Third, was it of pragmatic value to musicians? Unless these questions are addressed, the interpretation of the sources themselves and their connection to practice remain somewhat superficial, leading often to egregious conclusions.

To begin answering the first question, we must realize that "secondary" rhetoric, the study of stylistics, was a widely disseminated educational tool. Those theorists who imported it in any fashion that can be construed as systematic obviously believed in its efficacy. They thought they were saying something useful to somebody—but the question is, to whom? Even if their intentions were misguided, their motives are clear. All the same, we must not allow enthusiasm over new discoveries to blind us to the shortcomings of their approach. I am inclined to surmise that a great part of *Figurenlehre* was the result of rote learning by very young pupils—hence, rote teaching in the

---

[11](London and Washington, 1980), vol. 15, pp. 793-803.
[12]"*Ut oratoria musica*: the Rhetorical Basis of Musical Mannerism," in *The Meaning of Mannerism*, ed. F. W. Robertson and S. G. Nichols (Hanover, New Hampshire, 1972), pp. 37-65.

manuals. As one of my doctoral students said: "Burmeister is a teacher of the drill-sergeant mentality." He drilled his pupils in the figural tools for stylistic analysis to prepare them for the exercise of imitating masterpieces, and it seems the system, pedantic as it was, worked well enough. There is, by the way, some evidence that certain German composers published their youthful emulative efforts. My point is that Burmeister's and other theorists' justificatory references to the persuasive power of rhetorical language must not be mistaken for education programs aimed at focusing the responses of the listeners.

Furthermore, caution must also be exercised before imputing deep implications to every passing reference to rhetoric. Some of these are nothing more than fashionable slogans mustered to promote polemics or self-interest. The converse holds true for references to musical figures in writings on rhetoric. It is my view that the praises of the sweet delights of musical redundancy in the English sources discussed by Gregory G. Butler[13] represent defenses of ornate, periodic style in literature against the challenge posed by the newer fad of plain style in the early seventeenth century. Today these allusions carry no weight, given the victory of non-periodic prose. In the undergraduate essay manual used where I teach, it says: "Repetition in music is delightful; similar repetition in your essays is boring."

My other questions are interrelated, and they address the critical issue of the correlation between rhetorical analogies and compositional principles. We need to clarify the matter of theoretical intentions, especially whenever they seem confused in the sources. For example, in his article on the fantasia Butler provides strong evidence that in its written form this genre still used the improvised stereotype of sequential imitation, and his findings offer very original and important insights into the complex connection between *contrapunctus ex tempore* and *res facta*.[14] But I, for one, am not convinced that the fantasia was a musical image. Rather, commonplace sequential imitation *itself* becomes an

---

[13]"Music and Rhetoric in Early Seventeenth-Century English Sources," *Musical Quarterly* 66 (1980), 53-64.
[14]"The Fantasia as Musical Image," *Musical Quarterly* 60 (1979), 602-15.

image by rhetorical analogy to the faculty of practical judgment in the sensible soul. This explains why theorists considered any counterpoint smacking of routinized mechanics to be on a lower plane than learned counterpoint where intellection signaled the control of the reasonable soul. And in these stipulative statements, the rhetoric has very little to do with practical teaching. It is window dressing.

Gregory Butler's study of the fugue describes a grandiose metaphor espoused by so many theorists that it seems to render the fugue equivalent to dialectical persuasion.[15] I read this metaphor as descriptive rather than prescriptive. To assess its value for history of ideas, one must take into account the context of each writer in order to avoid misconstruing his terminology, premises, and goals. Impressive as conflation is in its coverage of so many sources, this method has its pitfalls. And when all is said and done, are there adequate grounds for assuming that the rhetorical concept played a major role in ensuring the vitality of the fugue? Would the fugue have flourished without it? Even if the answer to this question turns out to be "yes," we still have to find out why all these writers describe the fugue in rhetorical terms, and Butler has given us all much food for thought. To be bold in my turn, I hazard a guess. The analogy may have resulted from the logic of causal explanation and the episteme of mind. If fugue is to have a meaning, other than a dumb appeal to the lower instincts of the appetitive soul, then it communicates a discourse of musical ideas *analogous* to the cognitive imagination housed in the sensible soul and the rational judgment housed in the reasonable soul—and both are caused and effected primarily by the power of language. In the context of this philosophy, the only other alternative would have been to paraphrase Fontenelle, and ask: *"Fugue, que me veux-tu?"*

I pause here to say that in Gregory Butler's work and in the essays of Ursula and Warren Kirkendale, the erudition is so formidable and the ideas so refreshingly daring that to challenge their views on their own grounds requires an effort of equal stamina and magisterial scope. In the remaining space, I can only mention some questions that occur to me.

[15]"Fugue and Rhetoric," *Journal of Music Theory* 21 (1977), 49-109.

Warren Kirkendale has proposed a solution to a long-standing enigma: the origins of the imitative ricercar.[16] The points I make here do not negate the positive evidence unearthed by his research; they merely suggest there is some negative or inconclusive evidence as well. That the genre acted as a prelude to ensuing pieces does and evidently did suggest analogies to the *exordium* of oratory. The *exordium,* however, was not a discrete entity to be inserted before another separate unit, and perhaps this is why Cicero's advice to put in the *exordium* the main theme of one's speech does not tally with our uncertainty as to the thematic unity of individual pieces and their preludial ricercars. One must also consider whether etymology is veridical for either the improvisatory or the imitative ricercar. For example, the insinuative behavior of early ricercars does correlate with parts of Cicero's description of the *insinuatio,* but is this observation a workable causal explanation for the appearance of such pieces? In view of the works by composers connected by Kirkendale to Bembo's Ciceronian circle, one must further ask how long this phase lasted. For the more articulate the ricercar, the less like an *insinuatio* it is. Brian Vickers, an historian of rhetoric, wonders if Cicero's concept of the *insinuatio* as an indirect way of stealing into the hearts of hostile listeners applies to musical audiences.[17] I wonder if in its initial phase the ricercar was not intended primarily for the enjoyment of performers? If it was, the initial premise of parallels between the effects of *insinuationes* and ricercars on audiences is false. If not, are we still evaluating the insinuative ricercar by the standards of the fugue and, like baroque musicians, assessing it as an exemplar of *stile antico?* Would a sixteenth-century listener have judged the imitative principle of the ricercar as particularly insinuative?

As Warren Kirkendale told me, his article is an *exordium* to his wife's study of Bach's *Musical Offering.*[18] Those of us who were privileged to hear her paper last year also heard an excellent exchange of scholarly

---

[16]"Ciceronians versus Aristotelians in the Ricercar as Exordium," *Journal of the American Musicological Society* 32 (1979), 1-44.
[17]Paper read at the biennial conference of the International Society for the History of Rhetoric (Madison, Wisconsin, 1981).
[18]Ursula Kirkendale, "The Source for Bach's *Musical Offering,*" *Journal of the American Musicological Society* 33 (1980), 99-141.

opinions with Christoph Wolff. What I found interesting was that the discussion revolved around the assumption that the *Musical Offering* is a seriated cycle. Ursula Kirkendale sets out to prove that the correct order follows in every detail the eight parts of forensic oration given by Quintilian, and consequently that the musical style of each member finds its explanation in this source. Her arguments on behalf of this reading are extremely forceful, and I am sure the stature of her conception can withstand a few cavils. After all, Bach owned a copy of the treatise; he was knowledgeable in rhetoric; he left some clues for extra-musical references in the work itself; and he used symbolic devices elsewhere.

The main problem, as I see it, comes down to nagging inconsistencies arising from a rather extreme heuristic method. Why did Bach not choose the epideictic format, a more suitable one for a royal encomium? For the five diverse canons assigned to the *narratio longa* did Bach really ferret out the five epideictic virtues and the five forensic qualities, along with Homeric gods and heroes, from so many different chapters in a twelve-part book? How does one account for the imputed depiction of Homeric characters not mentioned by Quintilian? Did Bach's symbolism extend to such minuscule matters, and if it did, why did he not notice that according to Quintilian the *insinuatio* was reserved for difficult or scandalous subject matter in the law courts? If the regal recipient of this act of homage was supposed to be amused by a graphic musical projection of Tydeus, the puny but brave warrior, what was he to make of the *insinuatio?* To be sure, such quibbles do not demolish Ursula Kirkendale's main thesis. At the same time, her proposition as to the order of the cycle, which stands apart from hermeneutics, can be defended from evidence that has nothing to do with rhetorical considerations.

To encapsulate the general issue of methodology, the problem here is similar to the one I outlined for symbolism. The conflating of evidence from history of ideas, no matter how well documented, does not of its own accord establish symbolic or rhetorical intentions in music. In some cases, the relationship is too vague to be helpful. In others, making a series of one-for-one connections seems to invite microscopic incongruities. Neither of these drawbacks can be disregarded, for they raise doubts about the premises that called them into play. We simply have to keep chipping away at these boulders, and in preparing this paper I learned some valuable lessons about methods that induce me to be more self-critical. What I have learned is that we must develop incisive and historically accurate interpretations of the philosophical and epistemological premises behind verbal discourse on music and musical practices as well as similar premises behind their relationship, if any. The development of these tools will enhance our work not only as musicologists but also as humanists. I remain convinced that the application of history of ideas will continue to be a worthwhile endeavor, as we cooperate in refining our premises and methodology. We can turn limitations into opportunities. As Quintilian put it: *Sequitur emendatio, pars studiorum longe utilissima.*[19]

---

[19] *Institutio oratoria* X.iv.1.

Sketch Studies

Joseph Kerman

In September 1970 the International Musicological Society ran a five-day colloquium on nineteenth-century music at Saint-Germain-en-Laye. Each day was devoted to a different special topic; and the one that generated by far the greatest interest was "Problèmes de la création musicale au XIX⁰ siècle." Three prepared papers were submitted, rather than one as on each of the other days, and the discussion as recorded in *Acta musicologica* ran on and on for sixty pages—nearly twice as long

Musical sketches and autographs are occupying an ever larger place, particularly in recent dissertations. **Joseph Kerman,** Professor of Music at the University of California, Berkeley, edits the journal *19th-Century Music*, which has particularly encouraged studies in compositional process. His own *Autograph Miscellany from circa 1786 to 1799: Kafka Sketchbook* (London, 1970) won the Kinkeldey Prize of the American Musicological Society for 1970.

53

as for any of the other four topics.[1] Reading these papers and the responses to them in *Acta,* one sees articulated all the problems that are still occupying musicologists who work in this general area today. But one also realizes with some sense of shock how much the field has grown since 1970 and, in retrospect, how little published work was actually available to those pioneer colloquium participants. Even their own landmark essays had not yet appeared at the time of the meeting—or if they had, the publications were so recent they had scarcely been digested. Less than a dozen years later, it is not too much to say that we are surveying a different field.

If this field is called not the study of "création musicale" but simply "sketch studies," emphasis is shifted onto the materials of the research rather than its presumed goal, onto its methodology rather than its ideology. This seems to me preferable, though either way we are faced with some terminological imprecision. Not all work on composers' sketches and drafts is directed to an understanding of creation, creativity, or compositional process; nor is all work on compositional process restricted to sketches—even if the term "sketch" is stretched hard (perhaps inadmissibly hard) to include all kinds of composers' working documents. The important thing is to define or conceive the field broadly enough so that nothing is shut out in a way that is arbitrary to the material or inimical to a comprehensive view of it. A broad definition would cover all kinds of research, then, on a broad range of documents: sketches, drafts, working autographs, reject sheets, collettes (or paste-overs). This includes everything, in fact, that fulfills two conditions: (1) it has survived, and (2) it was in the composer's mind superseded. One would not in principle exclude the floor sweepings of electronic music studios.

Indeed, in practice sketch research blends imperceptibly and interestingly into the study of early versions, that is, early completed versions of works that were revised and hence superseded later, even though at first this may never have been intended or foreseen by the composer. We may seem to be crossing an important line here, for composers never think of their sketches as in any sense final or

[1]*Acta musicologica* 42 (1970), 32-78; and 43 (1971), 125-42, 142-44.

completed, as they do, temporarily, of their early versions. But this temporary finality begins to blur as we think of autographs that are altered, sometimes extensively, and of proof corrections and modifications made in later impressions or editions. This is not the place to probe the difficult concept of "finality" as applied to a piece of music, conceived of as a score or as sound, nor the equally difficult concept of "intention" as attributed to a composer. We need only remark that one whole substantial class of questions can be addressed similarly to sketches, drafts, and early ostensibly completed versions: questions about composers' criticism of their own music. And of course sketches may exist for those later versions of completed compositions, as well as for the early versions.

Early versions have long been the province of the editors of scholarly editions. In their *Revisionsberichte* these editors have always grappled with the difficult concepts alluded to above. And even before the age of musicology there was a lively interest in sketches, or at least drafts—a strictly practical interest in getting them reconstructed into music that could be performed and published. This interest has by no means lapsed; the line runs from Mozart-Stadler and Beethoven-Diabelli to Mahler-Cooke and Berg-Cerha. Charles Rosen, Raymond Lewenthal, and no doubt others are now playing the Schumann *Fantasie* with a da capo of the "An die ferne Geliebte" citation at the end of the last movement—just as it exists all crossed out in the *Stichvorlage*, a circumstance first made known in 1979.[2] (A great improvement, may I say.)

However, from the time of Gustav Nottebohm, sketches and drafts have been approached less frequently with reconstruction in mind than in the hope of learning something from them. Learning just what is a question we shall come to in a moment. Despite the well-known and greatly admired example of Nottebohm (his two main Beethoven sketchbook surveys of 1865 and 1880 were translated into English as recently as 1976), this branch of musicological study has not flourished until our own time, starting in the early-middle 1960s. And it has

[2] Alan Walker, "Schumann, Liszt and the C major Fantasie, Op. 17: a Declining Relationship," *Music & Letters* 60 (1979), 156-65.

flourished particularly in America. Although major work has of course been done elsewhere—Verdi sketches and drafts, for instance, were first investigated by Italian, English, and German scholars, as appears from the IMS colloquium—the concentration of this activity in this country is striking. Without wishing to press large claims for American musicology, I think we can see sketch studies as one of our recent distinctive contributions.

One center of it is or was Princeton, where if I am not mistaken the original impetus came from abroad, as a result of Oliver Strunk's close friendship with Erich Hertzmann, an enthusiastic sketch researcher in his later years. Another impetus from abroad, less localized, was that of Schenker. This was probably transmitted primarily by Oswald Jonas, who had followed Schenker in publishing studies of Beethoven sketches. As early as 1961, Allen Forte came out with his remarkable (though as I think misguided) Schenkerian analysis of some sketches for the Sonata in E major, opus 109, *The Compositional Matrix*. In 1970, the bicentennial year, there was quite a flood of Beethoven sketch publications issuing from this country. A gesture toward formalizing or institutionalizing the new discipline was made around that time, with the establishment of *Beethoven Studies* by Lewis Lockwood, Alan Tyson, and myself. This peripatetic serial—the third volume has just appeared[3]—invites mostly (if not exclusively) contributions dealing with sketch problems. (Tyson is British, needless to say, but his musicological orientation is really less native than American.) It was only on the basis of this Anglo-American initiative that German scholars at the Bonn Beethovenhaus reentered the field seriously, as they have now done with impressive results. Meanwhile an elegant and exhaustive bibliographical analysis of the Beethoven sketchbooks has been prepared by Tyson with two younger American scholars, Douglas Johnson (who edits the book) and Robert Winter.[4]

While there is no way to avoid saying a good deal about Beethoven in a paper on the present topic, I should prefer to minimize this as much as

[3]Ed. Alan Tyson (Cambridge University Press, 1982).
[4]*The Beethoven Sketchbooks,* to be published in 1983 by the University of California Press, Berkeley and Los Angeles (California Studies in 19th-Century Music, II).

possible. For one of the striking things about the recent American development is its avid embrace of other composers. Beethoven scholarship is the model; but everyone must surely understand the ways in which this model may suggest false analogies and raise false hopes. Here is a comparison that will tell it all: when Rufus Hallmark was writing his dissertation on *Dichterliebe,* he had for his material no more than two drafts, one of them partial, whereas Lewis Lockwood, studying a single Beethoven song ("Sehnsucht"), could draw on twenty-four.[5] In any case, it is now standard procedure to introduce a sketch article or monograph on a new composer with a disclaimer of parallels with the Beethoven situation, along with the customary obeisance toward Beethoven scholarship. Research that has come to my attention through articles, dissertations, and papers read at meetings of the American Musicological Society involves at least twenty composers and considerably more scholars—Bach, Mozart, Haydn, Rossini, Schubert, Schumann, Berlioz, Mendelssohn, Chopin, Liszt, Wagner (an especially important body of work), Verdi (despite the fact that his drafts are still kept under lock and key), Strauss, Debussy, Mahler, Stravinsky, Schoenberg, Berg, Webern, and Tippett. And of course more Beethoven. Then there was Jessie Ann Owens's paper last year about Cipriano de Rore. Who would have thought of sketches surviving from *that* period? It just goes to show that if you know what you are looking for, you may find it.

What can we learn from all these sketch studies? First of all, a wealth of factual information that is not obtainable in other ways. Beethoven's ambitious scena and rondo "Primo amore," WoO 92, was not written "ca. 1795-1800" in Vienna under Salieri's tutelage but ca. 1790-92 in Bonn, and originally to German words. Wagner determined the basic key scheme of *Götterdämmerung* before he wrote *Das Rheingold* or even dreamed (in E-flat) of doing so. In *Don Carlos,* Act V, the soprano air for Elisabeth was originally conceived in part for the tenor, Carlos. Berlioz sometimes used figured-bass notation in his sketches, just like

⁵Rufus Hallmark, *The Genesis of Schumann's Dichterliebe* (Ann Arbor: UMI Research Press, 1979); Lewis Lockwood, "Beethoven's Sketches for *Sehnsucht* (WoO 146)," *Beethoven Studies* [1], ed. Alan Tyson (New York, 1973), pp. 97-122.

his more academic (or less anti-academic) colleagues. If Webern had lived to finish the cantata that was to have been op. 32, it appears he would have used the combinatorial row with a new symmetrical pattern of octave transpositions.[6] One is constantly surprised not only by the number but also by the many different *kinds* of facts that are turned up in this line of work. Students investigating the sketches of some composer for the first time often seem overwhelmed, even seduced, by this factual cornucopia.

After these hard facts have been ascertained—and of course, a splendid network of technical expertise is needed for the ascertainment: tracking the sketches down, scrutinizing the paper, deciphering the notations, and making musical and historical sense out of them—a possible next step is for scholars to put them together and start investigating what is often called "compositional process." I might remark parenthetically that this is a somewhat loaded term, carrying the suggestion of a seamless development in time almost akin to the unfolding we attributed to certain kinds of music; and that what sketches and drafts reveal is more accurately described as a series of "compositional stages," and tentative compositional stages, at that. However this may be, much ingenuity has been expended in discovering how individual works have passed through various stages to their final state, and explaining why; and by extension, to analyzing how their composers have worked as a matter of routine. By a further extension, one could go on to study musical creativity in general, at least in theory. Apparently, though, this has not been seriously attempted since the days of Max Graf and Frederick Dorian in the 1940s.

Once it has been established how a composition has passed through various stages to its final state, the curious researcher will wish to investigate what all this reveals about the final state itself. Here we step

---

[6]Ludwig van Beethoven, *Autograph Miscellany from circa 1786 to 1799 . . . (the Kafka Sketchbook)*, ed. Joseph Kerman (London, 1970), II, 283; Robert Bailey, "The Structure of the *Ring* and its Evolution," *19th-Century Music* I (1977), 48-61; Andrew Porter, "A Sketch for *Don Carlos*," *Musical Times* 111 (1970), 882-85; D. Kern Holoman, *The Creative Process in the Autograph Musical Documents of Hector Berlioz, c. 1818-1840* (Ann Arbor: UMI Research Press, 1980), pp. 243-44; R. Larry Todd, "The Genesis of Webern's Opus 32," *Musical Quarterly* 66 (1980), 581-91.

into an area of controversy. The issues were raised at the IMS colloquium in 1970, and more recently they have been put into hard focus by Douglas Johnson, whose article "Beethoven Scholars and Beethoven's Sketches" appeared in *19th-Century Music* in 1978, together with several rejoinders.[7] Drawing a sharp distinction between the use of sketch studies for biography on the one hand and analysis on the other, Johnson took a particularly dim view of the latter. Under "biography" he included everything that has been mentioned in this paper so far, from chronological data to information about composers' working methods. As for "analysis," which Johnson felt could not be aided by sketch studies, he made it clear he was conceiving that term quite narrowly. The models he referred to were Schenkerian.

That Johnson's co-workers would have received his views with pleasure was hardly to be anticipated. Their response to his article was in fact overwhelmingly negative. It is interesting, however, that none of them seems to have questioned one of his basic assumptions, namely that a major impetus felt by scholars engaged in sketch work is indeed the potential contribution of such work to analysis. As the field has grown, so has this impetus grown in importance. And it is certainly not restricted to Beethoven studies. This appears from the program of a new monograph series announced in 1980 by Lewis Lockwood, a series which might be regarded as a more comprehensive formalization of the field of sketch studies. Lockwood's title is "Studies in Musical Genesis and Structure." The books he will publish will "seek to combine a view of the genetic evidence with an analytic view of the finished composition"; they might even "serve as background reading for courses in analysis." In other words, sketch studies will aid analysis.

Johnson does not believe this, of course, and the questions he raises are serious ones. They touch a nerve: a raw nerve, perhaps, because it has been nudged so many times. It is worth stressing that the consensus among commentators who have considered the genesis of works of art as material for analysis and criticism is thumbs down on the whole idea. It is with some sense of paradox, then, that one sees so many of the same commentators engrossed in sketch materials themselves. Johnson, to

?2 (1978-79), 3-17, 270-79; and 3 (1979), 187-88.

begin with, has skimmed Beethoven's early sketches brilliantly for what he calls "biography," having redated or refined the dating of a long list of compositions, and he has also taken some deeper soundings which scarcely support his own pessimism about the "insight" that can emerge from sketch studies. The paradox goes back to Nottebohm, who explicitly disclaimed the value of sketches for elucidating what *he* called the "organic" power or "demon" of Beethoven's genius: the same Nottebohm who published those "Eroica" drafts which have fascinated musicians of all stripes for over a century. You cannot enjoy the "Eroica" if you insist on thinking of those drafts, intoned Tovey; as you listen to the symphony, "forget the sketches utterly, as Beethoven himself forgot them." But in the same breath Tovey eulogized the drafts as "wonderful documents recording the profound workings of a creative mind," and he returned repeatedly in his essays on other works to discuss drafts and early.versions which presumably should have been forgotten just as utterly. In a recent issue of the *Journal of the American Musicological Society,* Edward T. Cone quotes Tovey's caveat about the "Eroica" sketches with approval; then he turns right around and cites an early draft of a piece by Roger Sessions to help clinch an analytical point two pages later in his article. Less ambivalent, Eric Sams, in a review of Hallmark's *Dichterliebe* dissertation, remarks pungently: "If a draft is essentially expression or communication, then commentary had better concentrate on what comes out, not what went in." And finally here is Leonard B. Meyer, in his last book, *Explaining Music:* "Tracing the genesis of a musical idea or a composition from the first sketch through the finished work may be illuminating psychologically and biographically, but it is not the same as, and cannot be substituted for, serious analytic criticism."[8]

---

[8]Johnson, *Beethoven's Early Sketches in the Fischoff Miscellany, Berlin Autograph 28* (Ph.D. diss., University of California at Berkeley, 1978, reprinted in part under the same title by UMI Research Press, Ann Arbor, 1980); Nottebohm, *Zweite Beethoveniana* (Leipzig, 1887), pp. viii-ix (cited and transl. by Johnson in "Beethoven Scholars," p. 5); Tovey, *Essays in Musical Analysis*, vol. III: *Concertos* (London, 1936), pp. 4-5; Cone, "The Authority of Music Criticism," *Journal of the American Musicological Society* 34 (1981), pp. 9, 11-12; Sams, in *Musical Times* 122 (1981), 382—see also August Gerstmeier in *Musikforschung* 34 (1981), 500; Meyer, *Explaining Music* (Berkeley and Los Angeles, 1973), pp. 78-79.

Now, I think it is clear that this argument about the futility of sketch studies for analysis, serious analytic criticism, insight, enjoyment, communication—whichever term the particular writer fancies—is a special case of a broader, more fundamental proposition about the futility of musicology in general. We have all had to confront the view that "facts about music" are irrelevant to "the music itself," by which is meant (however vaguely) the music's aesthetic content. And once we have identified the sketch argument as simply a version of the broader one, it should be easier for us as musicologists to deal with it. Easier, at least, for some of us. No doubt at one extreme of the profession there are those who in their heart of hearts really accept this proposition, and who therefore make no explicit effort to link "facts about music" with aesthetic experience or insight. These scholars tend to avoid close consideration of individual works of art, preferring to study aspects of music history or occasionally music's role in social, intellectual, and cultural history. At the other extreme are scholars who tend to use history, culture, sociology, etc., as a way to help us in what we call (or ought to call) criticism.[9] This is an activity that includes, but is not restricted to, analysis or the consideration of music's structure. It is musicologists of the latter school who find much of value in composers' sketches.

"Can analysis lean heavily on sketches?", asks Philip Gossett in his essay on the "Pastoral" Symphony sketches;[10] and Gossett holds back just short of answering in the affirmative. Like any reasonable being, he agrees with Meyer that a study of a work's genesis cannot be substituted for its analysis; but he also insists on finding a middle ground that will preserve "the utility of sketches to criticism." The important thing to notice here is the shift from the term "analysis" to "criticism." For of course if analysis is defined as narrowly as Johnson, the Schenkerians, and so many other analysts define it, neither sketches nor musicology nor anything else outside the bare notes on the page have any relevance to it. That is a tautology. And it is a tautology that reflects badly on the

[9]See Kerman, "A Profile for American Musicology," *Journal of the American Musicological Society* 18 (1965), 61-69.
[10]Philip Gossett, "Beethoven's Sixth Symphony: Sketches for the First Movement," ibid. 27 (1974), 248-84.

currently overrated discipline of analysis. It does not reflect badly on sketch studies.

The prospect changes, however, if we shift our sights from analysis, narrowly conceived, to criticism. The critic is certainly interested in the structure of individual works; how could he or she be otherwise, in today's intellectual climate?[11] But critics are also, like Gossett, interested in the difficult question of the composer's intention. They are interested in the Heine poem that Schumann (poor old pre-Schenkerian Romantic that he was) wrote underneath the bare notes of *Dichterliebe;* they are even interested in the poems Schumann considered and rejected. They are interested in referentiality—in the Beethoven citations in Schumann's *Fantasie,* and the subtler allusions that all compositions make silently to others. Critics do not try to forget the "Eroica" drafts while remembering the symphony, any more than they think they should (or can) block out the symphony's title, in either its Consular or Imperial forms. And they are interested not only in single autonomous works, but also in the structure of a composer's *œuvre,* including the shadow structure of projects that he aborted in the sketch stage or metamorphosed into other projects. All this is not a matter of mere casual interest. Each of the points mentioned here and of course many others play in to critical interpretation, exegesis, and judgment.

Let me outline briefly one not atypical situation that may develop in the course of work on sketches for some composition. The documents reveal a major problem that the composer has isolated and taken clear steps to deal with. Mendelssohn tried to make *Fingal's Cave* less "learned," less contrapuntal. Debussy tried to make *Pelléas et Mélisande* less Wagnerian, in both musical language and musical structure.[12] Do composers always solve such problems so perfectly that no traces of them remain in the final work? All composers? All the time? There were four different "final versions" of *Fingal's Cave.* What

---

[11]See Kerman, "How We Got into Analysis, and How to Get Out," *Critical Inquiry* 7 (1980), 311-31.

[12]R. Larry Todd, "Of Sea-Gulls and Counterpoint: the Early Versions of Mendelssohn's *Hebrides* Overture," *19th-Century Music* 2 (1979), 197-213; and Carolyn Abbate, "*Tristan* in the Composition of *Pelléas,*" ibid. 5 (1981), 117-41.

happened with these particular works was, we may suspect, something more interesting, if less perfect: a residue of the compositional problem remained in the final work of art as a conflict or tension. The tension contributes something distinct to its aesthetic quality, as the composer may very well have appreciated.

The argument that such tensions could, in theory, be perceived by an analyst examining the final works alone, without reference to the sketches, the composer's letters, etc., has no practical merit. The fact is that the observations in question were made by musicologist-critics working with sketches, R. Larry Todd and Carolyn Abbate. Sketch studies focus our understanding of a work of art by alerting us to certain specific points about it, certain points about it that worried the composer. So long as we do not fall into the trap of assuming they are the *only* points that worried or interested him, nothing but good can come of accepting such assistance as he has unwittingly provided us in the task of coming to understand his music. This thought or something close to it has already been articulated in Gossett's essay—and notice for a second time, in this quotation, the seemly switch from "analysis" to "criticism":

> Our understanding of a work of art is constantly in flux. . . . Whether or not we wish to invoke for a specific analysis information garnered from sketches, they affect both our more general understanding of the work and the kinds of questions we ask about related works. That an omniscient critic might perceive without assistance everything of significance knowable about a given work, whatever such knowledge might consist in, is irrelevant until such a critic appears.[13]

As historians we believe that finding the right analysis for a piece or a repertory is itself a subject for historical investigation. We should not leave any obvious stones unturned in this investigation, any more than we do in any other line of musicological inquiry.

Let me conclude with one or two observations of a more personal nature, concerning the ambience of sketch studies. The Mendelssohn and Debussy papers just referred to are not directed solely to analysis or

[13]Gossett, p. 261.

criticism. They also deal at some length with questions of paleography, chronology, and compositional process, and in this they are entirely characteristic. They combine what are now coming to be called the techniques of "hard" and "soft" musicology: for the isolation and separation of various stages of sketch study, as was proposed earlier in this paper, while useful for purposes of discussion, is arbitrary in terms of actual research practice. The stages merge smoothly and naturally into one another. They also merge, as was also pointed out earlier, into the broader study of composers' revisions. This field as a whole, it seems to me, allows for the deployment of the resources of musicology in the most comprehensive, and therefore the most powerful, fashion.

Sketch work, as my long list shows, is always directed to major composers, and typically to major works by them. I do not see how this can be interpreted other than as a trend in American musicology toward a more critical orientation, such as I have long advocated, even though some eminent sketch authorities have held back from pursuing their material beyond the strictly factual stage and others have concentrated hard on problems of methodology. Indeed, some scholars have started out with sketch research on major composers and then moved on to investigate other aspects of their subject. By the application of an approved "hard" discipline they have earned their spurs and, much more important, gained control and authority that allows them to pursue broad historical, stylistic, or critical questions in which sketches may play no large part. Let us note, also, the obvious fact that for obvious reasons the great majority of the major composers in question come from the nineteenth and twentieth centuries. The session at Saint-Germain-en-Laye on "Problèmes de la création musicale" formed part of a colloquium on nineteenth-century music. The recent trend in American musicology toward work in the nineteenth century has been mentioned frequently—more frequently than the trend toward criticism. The upsurge of sketch studies is part and parcel of both trends, which in any case run very closely parallel.

As is now clear, I am sure, my own interest in this whole question is as much practical as theoretical, as much political as philosophical. Edward Cone, in his admirable essay on "The Authority of Music

Criticism," distinguishes on primarily functional grounds between the "critic proper" and the "teacher-critic," by which he means the teacher of composition or of musical performance. To Leo Treitler we owe the powerful argument that Cone's "critic proper" is, in fact, the historian.[14] Let us not lose touch with the common ground occupied by all these critics. The teacher of composition, like the composer himself, is constantly dealing with questions of good and bad, good and better. It may be true that some sketch researchers work (and at meetings of the American Musicological Society, talk) in a very simplistic way, tracing with laborious innocence the sort of corrections that teacher-critics deal with every day in undergraduate composition courses. But such courses are not always on the required list for musicologists. We are the worse for it. I view with equanimity a subfield of musicology, sketch studies, in which the practitioners are constantly confronting not only questions of right and wrong, but also questions of good and bad, good and better.

[14]Leo Treitler, "History, Criticism, and Beethoven's Ninth Symphony," *19th-Century Music* 3 (1980), 193-210.

An expanded version of the following essay appears as " 'To Worship that Celestial Sound:' Motives for Analysis," *Journal of Musicology* I/2 (1982), 153-70. Used by permission.

Structural and Critical Analysis

Leo Treitler

I shall take my lead from our chairman's propaedeutic for this panel. The first of the questions that he asked us to address is, "How has the methodology contributed to our *understanding of the music and musical cultures of the past?*" (The emphasis is mine.) This way of putting the question implies a new conception of the task of music history, a radical departure, in fact, from the program that Guido Adler had set upon our profession in 1911: to trace the development of

Leo Treitler, Professor of Music at the State University of New York at Stony Brook, has educated all of us with his articles on the nature of history and criticism. (See, for example, "Musical Analysis in an Historical Context," *College Music Symposium* 6 [1966], 75-88; and "On Historical Criticism," *Musical Quarterly* 53 [1967], 188-205.) He was asked to consider where musicologists are or should be heading in their efforts at analysis and criticism.

musical style.[1] One hint of the newness of it is in the fact that as recently as 1972, during the Copenhagen congress of the International Musicological Society, a panel that was somewhat parallel to my portion of this one was entitled "Current Methods of Stylistic Analysis."[2] Not only the title is significant, but also the fact that the panel ignored it, for the most part.

The simple formulation of our task as the understanding of the music and musical cultures of the past can be read without surprise, because it catches the spirit in which many musicologists are now working. As for Adler's program, it seems to function mainly in the textbook industry in this country, sustained more by the market than by a shared belief that it represents the appropriate goals for musicology today. There is of course an interesting question about how that squares with the teaching of analysis.

II

I see no way of discussing the fit of analytical methodologies to the task of understanding the music of the past without first taking a measure of the task itself. Does the wording suggest that the "pastness" of our objects distinguishes our kind of inquiry from that of other groups of scholars dealing with music? It quickly becomes apparent that all music, except that which has not yet been composed, or performed, or thought of, is music of the past. On the other hand all music, insofar as it is or might be the object of the historian's attention, is in the historian's present as tradition. But tradition is the transmission of music through a continuous succession of presents or contemporary contexts (*Gegenwarten*), from the initial present of its moment of creation or first sounding, to the historian's present. There is naturally a priority of interest in that initial present, and that is presumably what is meant when we say, simply, that we are interested in the music *of the* past. But that priority is not sustained. It isn't the pastness of our objects

[1]*Der Stil in der Musik*, vol. I (Leipzig, 1911).
[2]*International Musicological Society: Report of the Eleventh Congress, Copenhagen 1972,* ed. Henrik Glahn, Soren Sorensen, and Peter Ryom (Copenhagen, 1974), I, 43-130.

that distinguishes them as "historical," or us as "historians." It is our interest in them as objects (or acts) in tradition.

So, not music *of* the past, as a principle of selection, but music *in* the past, music in contexts, as a principle of knowlege. History is a discipline, not by virtue of a particular subject matter, but by virtue of an epistemological stance. And the change in the formulation of the task of music history entails most centrally a change in epistemology, a shift of emphasis from the genetic to the ontological.

The difference turns on the question of what it is to *understand* the music of the past, particularly on the matter of *context* again. There is a causal, positivist sense in which music is understood as a precipitate of its context. And there is a hermeneutic sense, in which it is viewed as a meaningful item within a wider context of practices, conventions, assumptions, transmissions, receptions—in short a musical culture, which serves to endow its constituent aspects with meaning while attaining its own meaning from the combination of its constituents. Like historians of literature and art, we are becoming more interested in contexts of meanings than contexts of causes. That has consequences for the role of analysis—both in its absolute importance and in its particular tasks—and for the methodologies that will be suited to them.

From this perspective analysis must be a central activity of the historian. The most engaged and engaging writing about the music of the past nowadays tends increasingly toward a comprehensive understanding. There is a tendency to want to understand, not just the structure of the musical object, but the meaning of its structure, interpreted as a conception against the background of norms and models, stylistic and semiotic codes, expectations and reactions, aesthetic ideals, circumstances of transmission and reception. Not just the score is evidence for such analysis, but the scores of other music, manuscript traditions, evidence about performance practice, the writings of theorists and pedagogues, read in understanding of the nature of *their* tasks, *their* readerships, and the style of their reasoning; critical writing, chronicles, and more. What I am talking about is the crossroads of approaches that, in the nineteenth century, were called hermeneutics and historicism, before those words, especially the second, became accusations. With such a notion about his task, the historian will not sensibly tolerate the separation of "analytical" from "historical" methodologies, even in the sense of the sequence of investigative operations. As investigative procedures, neither analytical nor historical methods can be absolutely prior to the other. They inform one another in a continuous circle.

The polemical sense with which the term "historicism" is now loaded has several factors behind it. One of them is also among the issues that have divided analysis and history and their practitioners. It is the absolute priority that historicism once wished to give to the initial context of its objects in studying them. The nineteenth-century hermeneuts (specifically Schleiermacher and Dilthey) essentially accepted that notion. According to its original definition, hermeneutics is the art of clarifying and mediating by the intepreter's own efforts what is encountered in tradition. That meant bridging the gap between the familiar world of the present and the strange world of the past. The nineteenth-century hermeneuts held the interpreter's boundedness in his present as something to be transcended. Bridging the distance between minds meant shedding the interests and habits of the present in order to understand the subjective intentions of the persons who are involved in history.

In this century the philosopher Hans-Georg Gadamer and his followers have given systematic and reasoned legitimation for the reluctance of critics in all the arts to restrict their analytical categories to those that might be recognized by the artist, without opening the way to utter relativism.[3] The work of art is regarded, not as a fixed and passive object of study, but as an inexhaustible source of possible meaning. It exists in tradition, and the effort at understanding it is episodic; every understanding is a moment in the life of tradition, but also in the life of the interpreter. Like language, art bears the history of past understandings. The interpreter confronts not the work alone, but the

[3]Gadamer's major work is *Wahrheit und Methode* (Tübingen, 1975); English trans. ed Grarrett Barden and John Cumming, *Truth and Method* (New York, 1975). An excellen introduction to Gadamer's thought is provided by the editor of the collection of essays published under the title *Philosophical Hermeneutics,* trans. and ed. David E. Linge (Berkeley and Los Angeles, 1976).

work in its effective history ("Wirkungsgeschichte"). The encounter is more a conversation with a respondent than an operation on a passive object. The interpreter's knowledge and interest are as much factors in understanding as are the meanings of his objects in their successive contexts. Understanding takes place in the fusion of the horizons of present and past.

With these very brief remarks about aesthetic and historical knowledge I have said what I can here about what is suggested to me by the expression "understanding the music and musical culture of the past," the meaning of which I, at least, have not found to be as self-evident as might appear at first.

III

Do we currently have, in musical analysis, methodologies that lead to the understanding of the music of the past?

Ian Bent has given us, in his fine article in *The New Grove,* an overview of analytical methodologies, as well as a history of the practice of musical analysis.[4] On the history we also have a number of recently published separate studies, the most valuable of which is Ruth Solie's paper "The Living Work: Organicism and Musical Analysis," in last year's *19th-Century Music.*[5] (The one thing I wonder about is the title; I'll say why later.) And we shall soon have Allan Keiler's book on Heinrich Schenker.[6] From all of them we can learn something about the historical and theoretical factors that underlie the characteristics of analytical methodologies as they are.

The analysis of music as such goes back little more than a century. Before then, concrete demonstrations about how things musical worked were conceived more as models for composition. Thus they had the aspect of taxonomies or inventories of correct practice. The philosophical pivot for the emergence of an analytical attitude was provided by the aesthetic idea, since the eighteenth century, of the

[4]Article, "Analysis," *The New Grove Dictionary of Music and Musicians* (London, 1980), I, 340-88.
[5]*19th-Century Music* 4 (1980), 147-56.
[6]Cambridge: Harvard University Press, forthcoming.

contemplation of beauty for its own sake, and without self interest (especially in the writing of Immanuel Kant). In contrast to the tradition of cataloguing correct practices, what characterized aesthetic writing in general and analytical writing about music in particular during the nineteenth century was a preoccupation that had two sides: reflection about the nature of the creative process, and the search for structural coherence in music. These were not abstract, scientific interests; they were motivated by ideologies about the human faculty of genius and the quality of greatness in music, for which structural unity was the *sine qua non*. There is an evaluative impulse in analysis from the beginning, and that impulse survives in the seductive pleasure that can attend the discovery of a potent connection, an analytical closure, and thereby distract the historian from his real task of interpretation.

The relationship between the idea of genius and unity is this: genius is the natural creative capacity of mind that provides the controlling force in the production of unified works of art. This doctrine was couched in terms appropriated from the organicist philosophy of the early nineteenth century, and the organic metaphor was applied to all the elements of it: the human mind, the capacity of genius, the creative process, and the work of art. The standard of greatness could be thought of as an idealized model of structured process, and the analysis of music as the uncovering of deep-seated principles of organization on the basis of such a model; or, to put it in other words, the deductive explanation of the work from such a model.

The analytical methodologies that Bent surveys in his detailed review fall into two general categories. On one hand there are empirical, discovery-procedure approaches, such as the feature analysis entailed in Jeppesen's *Palestrina and the Style of the Dissonance*,[7] Jan LaRue's *Guidelines for Style Analysis*,[8] and countless computer-assisted analytical projects. And on the other hand there are the essentially deductive procedures based on models of structural process, such as Riemann's phrase-structure analysis, the various approaches in the tradition of *Formenlehre*, Réti's thematic process analysis and its

[7]New York and London, 1946.
[8]New York, 1970.

descendant, serial analysis, and Schenker's structural analysis. It is the methodologies in this second category, which grew out of the organicist movement of the nineteenth century, that seem to predominate in the teaching of analysis today.

We can see in some of the most characteristic features of these methodologies and the analyses that they generate, the marks of their ideological origins. First, the point of view is holistic and unitarian. The work must be explicable in terms of a single principle, and every detail must be derivable from the idea of the whole. Second, the focus is mainly on pitch structures. It is in the analysis of pitch structures that theorists have most successfully demonstrated the properties of organic coherence. On the other hand other dimensions of music, in which organic structure is less handily demonstrated, have come in for relatively little attention: time, sound qualities (sonority, register, timbre), the communication between performing roles, the relationship between music and language where there is a sung text. Third, the analytical perspective tends to be from the inside out, or from back to front, rather than from beginning to end. Music is apprehended as synchronic structure. (That is why I wondered about Ruth Solie's title, "The *Living* Work.") One who opposed that conception was Tovey, who preferred a "time-like" to a "map-like" view of music. The difference is fundamental. Analysis whose center of gravity is a synchronic conception of pitch structure is little interested in the phenomenology of music. Schenker's synchronic conception was an important theoretical achievement—in a way the final unfolding, so to speak, of the organic principle. But it has meant that the point of view of the auditor has not been much of a factor in the practice and teaching of analysis in this country. And that fact is now registered in the notice of the absence of a tradition of criticism in musical studies.

Fourth, analysis tends to be of an *a priori,* rationalist nature. It proceeds from universals about how music works, more than it seeks to discover how musics work. Finally, prevailing modes of structural analysis are anti-historical, in two respects: they decontextualize their objects in their rationalistic treatment of them; and they are taught and practiced without notice taken of their own historicality, or, in general, of the role that particular models play in the organization of understanding.

Now the one thing I do not intend with this characterization of analytical practice is that it should be taken as an indictment. That would be to fault analysis for failing to accomplish what it did not set out to accomplish. What I do mean to allege is that the two things I have tried to describe—historical understanding and formalist analysis—do not match very well. I think that is evident from a comparison of the descriptions in the abstract. But it is driven home by some accounts of music of the past that have been generated from the formalist point of view and that provide questionable or inadequate historical understanding.

One such account that has been of concern to me in my research is the general interpretation of the Gregorian Chant tradition that is represented by the characterization of chants in a widely read book on the subject as "unified works of art, no less so than in the case of a sonata by Beethoven."[9] This attributes to a Romantic aesthetic conception of dubious relevance, characteristics that are far better understood from the point of view of the context of generation, transmission, and function in which the tradition actually thrived. The misinterpretation here eventually touches all aspects of the subject.

Another is the succession of analyses of pitch structures in the second of Schumann's *Dichterliebe* songs to which Joseph Kerman called attention last year,[10] wherein three prominent analysts consistently ignore the fact that their object is a song, performed by a pianist and singer who respond to one another in particular ways that influence the perception of the pitch structure, with the singer singing a poem that itself has structure and meaning. The result, as Kerman showed, is an inadequate understanding, even of the pitch structure.

Still on the subject of the *Dichterliebe,* there is a published interpretation of the sixth song, "Im Rhein," in which the dotted rhythm of the piano figure is said to represent waves.[11] What is missed thereby is a reference to an item of a stylistic code—the Baroque

[9]Willi Apel, *Gregorian Chant* (Bloomington, 1958), p. 362.
[10]"How We Got Into Analysis, and How to Get Out," *Critical Inquiry* 7 (1980), 311-31.
[11]Eric Sams, *The Songs of Robert Schumann* (London, 1969), p. 112.

majestic style—and the reflection through that, so to speak, of the image of the Cologne Cathedral. And with that is missed an entry into the meaning of the song—a case of misinterpretation resulting from decontextualization.

The single-minded formalist habit of blocking out music-language relations brings me back to the music of the Middle Ages, which has suffered misinterpretation on a grand scale, in a way that is displayed in this representative statement taken from *Die Musik in Geschichte und Gegenwart:* "Medieval composers had no direct interest in their text; the correlation of tone and word remained haphazard. Almost any music could be composed to almost any words."[12] Virtually all the formalist attitudes are ultimately wrapped up in that assessment.

But more important than such gaffes—major or minor—are the blind spots of formalist analysis: *Formenlehre* in abundance, but little attention to time-process and time-sense; sophisticated theories of tonality, but little interest in the qualitative side of key relations, although this was an important matter for composers of the era of common practice. It was then an instrument for the rhetorical and expressive functions of music. But key relations in this qualitative sense have a sequential, narrative order that has to be played out in real time, even conceptually. It will not survive reduction to a synchronic representation. That means that what is a gain in theoretical understanding is a loss in historical understanding.

For Schenker, Gregorian chant and the music of Wagner were blind spots—he pronounced them both incoherent.[13] Here the analytical methodology constitutes a criterion for the admission of works into the

---

[12]Friedrich Blume, article "Renaissance," *Die Musik in Geschichte und Gegenwart* XI (1963), 276; trans. M. D. Herter Norton in part I of Blume, *Renaissance and Baroque Music* (New York, 1967), p. 75.

[13]The discussion of Gregorian chant occurs in Schenker's *Neue musikalische Theorien und Phantasien* of 1906, published in English as *Harmony,* trans. Oswald Jonas (Chicago, 1954). It is worth quoting some of his language: "Musical instinct, to begin with, was totally inartistic and only very gradually condensed and rose from a chaos of fog to a principle of art. . . . We have to accept the fact that the majority of Gregorian chants lacked any guiding principle, thus placing themselves outside the scope of art in the intrinsically musical and formally technical sense" (pp. 134-36). The discussion of Wagner occurs in *Das Meisterwerk in der Musik,* Band II (München, Wien, Berlin, 1926), "Fortsetzung der Urlinie-Betrachtungen," pp. 29-30.

canon. An interesting variant is presented by the case of Ockeghem. Judging from the language of much of this modern literature, his music, too, might be in danger of being declared incoherent: "Generalizations about [its] formal principles are difficult to formulate" because it "unfolds freely and in an ad hoc manner." "Il n'a pas de système." The music "avoids precisely those features that would enable the listener to grasp the details or the large structural units and to integrate them in his mind." The music has structure and order, but they are "disguised and inaudible." Or it is put the other way about: "there are masses with no consistent unifying device at all," but "the coherent effect [they make] on the listener is the result of internal consistency of style and expression." As one writer summarizes it, Ockeghem is "a difficult, even an enigmatic composer."

But Ockeghem's stature as a great master is a *donnée* that has come down through an almost unbroken tradition since his own day. How can that be squared with the fact that his music fails to meet the most important general criterion for greatness?

The historian's puzzlement over Ockeghem's music finally becomes transformed into one of its leading characteristics. His "far-reaching renunciation of rational organization" is the manifestation of a "musical mysticism." The suspicion that the image of Ockeghem as mystic comes, at least in part, as resolution of the paradox is fed by the fact that it is a response neither to concrete, positive features of the music, nor to any documented connections between Ockeghem and traditions of philosophical or theological mysticism. The term "mysticism" used with reference to Ockeghem has not been given any content. And the suspicion is further reinforced by the fact that the emergence of this image concides more or less with the forced abandonment of an earlier image of Ockeghem as paragon of the strict formalist art of imitative counterpoint.

This story illustrates the episodic and contingent nature of historical understanding. It demonstrates the role that formalist analytical attitudes play in the formation of such understanding. And it shows that they continue to exercise the biases of their organicist roots even after those have gone deep underground.

The obvious conclusion from these brief citations is that historical understanding is neither the prime target nor the chief beneficiary of the discipline of analysis. As music historians we want analytical methodologies that are less normative and more phenomenological and historical; that take account of much more than pitch structures; and that concern themselves not with structures alone, but with the relations of structure and meaning.

We might make a better beginning by trying to teach analysis along historical lines—not simply arranging the music for analysis in chronological order, but deriving methodologies as needed from the coordinated study of music, music theory and criticism, reception and transmission, performance practices, aesthetics, and semiotics. Such an enterprise would in most cases require the confrontation and collaboration of historians and theorists, and that would do no harm at all. On the contrary it might foster a more critical habit of mind in students, and it might be an influence toward reducing the deplorable rift that now exists in this country between music history and theory.

Iconography

James McKinnon

Those called upon in the past to speak on iconography as a musicological methodology have tended to follow one of two positions. The first stemmed from a rather uncritical optimism: according to it many of the hitherto impenetrable mysteries of early music will be solved once we gain access to massive repositories of iconographic evidence.[1] The second shared the optimism of the first but tempered it

[1]One still detects a vestige of this position in Walter Salmen, "The Value of Iconographical Sources in Musical Research," *Modern Musical Scholarship,* ed. Edward Olleson (London, 1980), pp. 206-14.

James McKinnon, Professor of Music at the State University of New York at Buffalo, has written several articles that are models of careful iconographic study: "Musical Instruments in Medieval Psalm Commentaries and Psalters" (*Journal of the American Musicological Society* 21 [1968], 4-20) and "Representations of the Mass in Medieval and Renaissance Art" (*Journal of the American Musicological Society* 31 [1978], 21-52) are two. He addresses recent trends and prospects for musical iconography.

with serious cautions on the limitations of iconographic evidence, for example the ignorance of the artist about precise musical detail, or the inability of his medium to portray it.[2]

This second is by no means an irresponsible one; it can and has given rise to creditable results. Nevertheless it presents theoretical problems, and in the most recent years a third position has begun to take its place. It is, if I may state it in rather extreme form, that there is something dubious about the entire enterprise of analyzing works of art as musicological evidence. The proper study of a work of art is the work of art itself, and any evidence it might produce for any historical discipline is purely incidental. It is a byproduct, and more than that a byproduct that will remain hidden precisely to those who in their anxiousness to obtain hard evidence fail to begin their search with a full and unbiased study of the work of art in question.[3]

Today, with your permission, I will attempt to supply a series of six specific points which follow from this general position. The first three are principles of evidentiary limitation, while the latter three are positive suggestions for the more promising future uses of musical iconography. In presenting these I make no claim for coverage of the entire field, especially with respect to chronology, where one might find a bias in favor of the medieval and Renaissance periods. Still less can I claim to set forth a definitive statement on the theory of musical iconography; any such theory must rest upon iconographic theory in general, a rich field which can be represented here but slightly.[4] And for a final limitation I concentrate solely upon the result of music iconographic research and omit all mention of the invaluable work of

[2]For a classic statement of this second position see Emanuel Winternitz, "The Visual Arts and the Historian of Music," *International Musicological Society: Report of the Eighth Congress, New York, 1961*, vol. I (Kassel, 1961), pp. 109-20; reprt. in Winternitz, *Musical Instruments and Their Symbolism in Western Art* (New York, 1967; New Haven, 1979), pp. 25-42.

[3]There are traces of the emergent position in the methodological observations of American musical iconographers especially. See the statements of Richard Leppert, Colin Slim, and the present author in the *RIdIM Newsletter* 2 (1977); and the introductory remarks of Howard Brown in the article "Iconography of Music," *The New Grove Dictionary of Music and Musicians* (London, 1980), IX, 11.

[4]I have in mind especially the work of the Warburg iconographers, Erwin Panofsky and Ernst Gombrich.

collection and organization undertaken by agencies such as the Répertoire International d'Iconographie Musicale. Nevertheless I would hope that my remarks are broadly applicable to the mainstream of musical iconography as practiced during the past several decades.

The first principle is implicit already in our introductory statement; it involves one's basic attitude in approaching a work of art as evidence.[5] We mentioned above the tendency of some to cite limitations on the use of iconographic evidence such as ignorance of the artist about musical detail or the inability of his medium to depict it. These limitations, which are occasionally set forth in lists of considerable length, are wise and salutary as far as they go. They can be based, however, upon an implicit fallacy, namely that we treat a work of art—let us use the term painting for convenience of exposition—as a photograph, albeit a defective one. That is to say that the painting is looked upon as a representation of reality, although one which admittedly fails to measure up for a variety of reasons. I would suggest that this is a reversal of the proper order of things brought about by our anxiousness to exploit the painting for evidentiary purposes. Rather a painting must first of all be viewed as an entity unto itself, in the same way that a musical composition, if you will, is an auditory entity unto itself, and not a reflective imitation of everyday sounds. To be sure, there is some sort of relationship between every painting and the external world, and our common sense tells us that in most cases this relationship is more direct and obvious than the relationship between a musical composition and the audible world. Nevertheless it is improper to assume the relationship. One begins with the thought that a painting represents itself, and that even many of its most realistic details might be dictated by the artist's compositional impulse. Its relationship to external reality, then, is one that must be established positively by a variety of means, such as a knowledge of the history of style, a knowledge of the

---

[5]These first three principles are also explained, occasionally in very similar language, in the author's "Fifteenth Century Northern Book Painting and the Performance of Liturgical Music," to be published by Cambridge University Press in the proceedings of a conference on fifteenth-century music held at New York University on 2-3 October 1981. The parallel explanations are made complementary to each other by the use of different illustrations.

history of iconographic types, a knowledge of the subject in question, and above all the employment of sound general historical method.

As an example we might take the study of the eminent pioneer musical iconographer Emanuel Winternitz, "On Angel Concerts in the 15th Century: A Critical Approach to Realism and Symbolism in Sacred Painting."[6] The study proceeds from the assumption that the elaborate angel consorts of Renaissance art have much to tell us about instrumental groupings of the period; whereas in reality it tends more to point out—with considerable astuteness, be it noted—the musical anomalies of the selected illustrations. One might say, then, that the study consists in the step-by-step dismantlement of its *raison d'être* and ask why it was written in the first place. This is speaking with the advantage of hindsight, however, and a fairer judgment is that the article is a responsible product of the second position described in the introductory remarks above. Today, however, one hopes that the musical iconographer who contemplates a study of Renaissance angel consorts would start with the assumption that their instrumental groupings were generally motivated by some artistic impulse or another, symmetry for example, and that they can be taken to reflect historical reality only in the presence of specific positive indications that this is the case. For example, there might be a literary source describing precisely the combinations pictured, or the painting in question might be an attempt to portray an actual historical event. But again such conditions must be demonstrated rather than assumed.

Our second principle is that which Ernst Gombrich called the "primacy of genres."[7] According to it the key step in the interpretation of a picture is the determination of its genre. Artistic genre is used in a somewhat more narrow sense than, say, a musical genre; it involves subject matter, medium, and even period—for example, the Crucifixion page of a medieval missal, a Renaissance pietà, or the Christ in Glory in the apse of a basilica. The identification of artistic genre has a two-fold purpose: it enables us to search efficiently for other examples of the

---

[6] *Musical Quarterly* 49 (1963), 450-63; reprt. in *Musical Instruments and Their Symbolism in Western Art,* pp. 137-49.
[7] *Symbolic Images* (London, 1972), p. 5.

genre and it aids in their interpretation once found. Perhaps the searching function can be taken as self-explanatory here,[8] so that we might turn immediately to an example of the interpretative function.

The miniature in plate IA is an illustration of Psalm 97, *Cantate domino canticum novum,* from a thirteenth-century English psalter. One notes with curiosity what appears to be a crutch under the arm of a clerical singer; its explanation, however, is obvious to one familiar with the history of the genre.[9] The group of singing clerics at the lectern became the standard illustration of Psalm 97 in English psalters during the mid-thirteenth century. It replaced the earlier thirteenth-century English illustration of Psalm 97, the Annunciation of the Shepherds (see plate IB), in which the shepherds are greeted by the "new song" that the angels sang at Christmas, *Gloria in excelsis.* Subsequent English illumination was slow to abandon the theme entirely, and it seems clear enough that the cleric's crutch of plate IA is a lingering shepherd's crook.

A quaint example, you might say, while wondering if it has anything to do with musical iconography. As a matter of fact, Werner Bachmann, the editor of *Musikgeschichte in Bildern,* displayed a series of pictures at the Berkeley meeting of the International Musicological Society which showed singers in a variety of manual gestures; he wondered what their musical significance might be.[10] It so happens that a strikingly large proportion of his pictures were thirteenth-century illustrations of Psalm 97, miniatures showing the three clerical singers at a lectern, such as that of plate IC. One familiar with the genre will suspect immediately that these gestures, rather than conveying subtle musical meaning, are simply carried over from the excited shepherds who hearken to the angelic song in the same way that the shepherd's crook was carried over. The artist, after all, must do something with the

[8]For an example of the searching function see fig. 2 and the accompanying commentary of the author's "Fifteenth Century Northern Book Painting."
[9]On the iconography of Psalm 97 see the author's "Canticum Novum in the Isabella Book," *Mediaevalia* 2 (1976), 207-22.
[10]"Probleme musikikonographischer Forschung und der Edition von Bildquellen" in *International Musicological Society: Report of the Twelfth Congress, Berkeley, 1977,* ed. Daniel Heartz and Bonnie Wade (Kassel, 1981), pp. 825-27.

Fig. Ia: *Cantate Domino*. Psalter; Oxford, All Souls College, Ms. 7, f. 89.

Fig. Ib: *Cantate Domino*. The Amesbury Psalter; All Souls College, Ms. 6, f. 112.

Fig. Ic: *Cantate Domino.* Psalter; Oxford. The Bodleian Library, Ms. Astor A.1., f. 127v.

Fig. Id: *Cantate Domino*. The Gorleston Psalter; London, The British Library, Ms. Add. 49622, f. 126.

singers' hands, and what could be more in keeping with the production of medieval illuminated books than to copy the hands of shepherds from previous illustrations of Psalm 97? We must be grateful for the illustration of Psalm 97 from the early fourteenth-century Gorleston Psalter (plate ID); it seems well-calculated to assist us in grasping this point with its two-tiered recapitulation of the history of the genre. Above we have the Annunciation of the Nativity to gesticulating shepherds; below, the three similarly-gesticulating singers.

Theoretically our third principle might be explained as a corollary to the first two. In its simple statement, however, it reads more like an observation than an *a priori* principle. It is that a great deal of the music historical information we derive from iconographic evidence consists in broad general conclusions based upon a long-range survey. For example, one looks with skepticism upon Jean Perrot's tendency to reconstruct individual Hellenistic organs by counting and measuring their pipes; while on the other hand one is perfectly comfortable with its broad conclusion about the general size and appearance of the Hellenistic organ, and the operation of its hydraulic wind supply and of its keyboard mechanism.[11] To take a more positive example one is convinced, even if not surprised, in reading Howard Brown's survey of *trecento* angel music that the portative organ must have figured prominently in contemporary music; while one is both convinced of and surprised at the reality of dual-pipe playing during the period.[12] We note further the total absence of the transverse flute and the virtual absence of the recorder, the latter circumstance being one that will come as a great disappointment to some but comfort, perhaps, to others. If there is an apparent contradiction, incidentally, between this acceptance of evidence from *trecento* angel consorts and the earlier rejection of evidence from *quattrocento* consorts, it is only apparent. The distinction between the two is that the *quattrocento* study deals with instrumental groupings and the *trecento* study with individual instruments. Brown rejects at the outset the notion that the instrumental combinations

[11] *The Organ from its Invention in the Hellenistic Period to the End of the Thirteenth Century,* trans. Norma Deane (Oxford, 1971).
[12]"Trecento Angels and the Instruments They Play," *Modern Musical Scholarship*, pp. 112-40.

reflect reality and works rather with the sensible assumption that individual instruments—particularly when they are portrayed with great frequency during a period of relatively realistic style—must have been observed by artists in contemporary music making. Within that artistic milieu there is no other plausible explanation for their appearance.

One can multiply similar illustrations of the principle, particularly from the area of organology. It is another matter, however, with performance practice since the most obvious sort of evidence for performance practice would seem to involve instrumental combinations and hence to be subject to the strictures expressed above. Nevertheless, exceptions are possible so long as the proper circumstances are in place; ideally these would include a smaller ensemble, of plausible authenticity, which appears frequently in similar circumstances. The ensemble must be a small and a familiar one so that the artist can reproduce it as a single visual entity in the same way that he would reproduce a contemporary artifact. Edmund Bowles has given us a good example of this in the fifteenth-century combination of three *haut* wind instruments, say, two shawms and one *S*-shaped trumpet, which are seen again and again being played from minstrel galleries at weddings, balls, and other festive occasions at court.[13] An interesting performance-practice observation of a different sort is made by Craig Wright, to the effect that secular singing groups in fifteenth-century art, chanson performers perhaps, sang from notated scrolls or unbound sheets rather than from the elegant little *chansonniers* preserved today.[14]

To repeat the general principle, what we observe here are broad general conclusions based upon a substantial quantity of examples. There is, as I suggested above, a theoretical explanation behind this phenomenon, one which requires, however, a more lengthy exposition than is practical here. Allow me simply to suggest it, then, by a somewhat outrageous analogy. You will not observe the human figure

[13]For examples see *Musikleben im 15. Jahrhundert, Musikgeschichte in Bildern,* III, 8 (Leipzig, 1977), figs. 1, 2, 29, 30, 33, 36, 41, and 42.
[14]"Voice and Instruments in Art Music of Northern France during the 15th Century: A Conspectus," *Report of the Twelfth Congress,* p. 644.

drawn in earlier medieval art to perfect proportion, but neither will you find it drawn with two heads, nor with three arms, although you might find it drawn with less than the proper number of fingers.

With these three interpretative principles in mind, we turn now to three points of a different nature, suggestions as to the most potentially fruitful areas of future musical iconographic research.

The first I would single out, to the surprise of my closest colleagues, I would imagine, is organology, the history of musical instruments. There is a measure of irony here. The Dark Ages of musical iconography were dominated by organology, and a large proportion of the early abuses of iconographic evidence was the work of organologists. Even more irritating to some of us was the presumption that organology and musical iconography were coterminous, whereas in truth organology is not even an iconographic subject in the proper sense; it is what Panofsky would have called, along with the study of artifacts in general, a pre-iconographic subject.[15]

Nevertheless, the fact of the matter is that, to the extent that one has in mind hard musicological information, organology appears to be the area in the best position to profit from the continued use of visual evidence. If there is a single chief reason for this, perhaps, it is that in many instances iconographic evidence is the only available organological evidence. In any case it is gratifying to see the recent more critical attitude among organologists which has replaced the earlier naiveté. Examples which come readily to mind are David Boyden's work on the violin,[16] Edwin Ripin's work on early keyboard instruments,[17] and Jeremy Montague's work on medieval instruments in general.[18]

My second suggestion, which will be dealt with very briefly, is that frequently we must be content, indeed positively happy, with

[15]See the author's application of Panofsky's iconographic terminology to musical iconography: "Musical Iconography: A Definition," *RIdIM Newsletter* 2 (1977), 15-18.
[16]*The History of Violin Playing from its Origins to 1761* (London, 1965).
[17]For example, see "On Joes Karest's Virginal and the Origins of the Flemish Tradition," *Keyboard Instruments, Studies in Keyboard Organology, 1500-1800,* ed. Edwin M. Ripin (Edinburgh, 1971), pp. 67-76.
[18]See, for example, Gwen and Jeremy Montague, "Beverly Minster Reconsidered," *Early Music* 6 (1978), 401-18.

iconographic evidence functioning as corroborative rather than independent evidence. Very often, for all the reasons suggested above, we are unwilling to give credence to the details of an early painting until they are verified by more solid evidence, say archival or literary evidence. One objects, however, that this is mere illustration, and I in turn would object to the word mere. The puritanical view of history which the first objection implies is fallacious; history, after all, is not what happened at one time, but our presentation of it. For example, a strikingly detailed and beautifully executed fifteenth-century miniature of Mass celebration in a court chapel is a genuine part of the historical record even if it presents no information which cannot be assembled from other sources.[19]

My third and final suggestion is that pride of place in music iconographic studies belongs to subjects which lie somewhat outside the mainstream of contemporary American musicology; I refer to areas like the social and cultural history of music, and the intellectual history of music. This follows from the simple circumstance that so large a proportion of the content of works of art with musical subject matter has relevance for categories of that sort rather than for the more conventional concerns of music history.[20] As an example one can cite the informal music-making emphasized by Walter Salmen in his volume *Musikleben im 16. Jahrhundert*—musical games, dances, carnivals, town musicians, military music, and the like.[21] Or one thinks of Reinhold Hammerstein's magisterial book on the music of angels,[22] a work, incidentally, which is much sounder in its overall presentation than it is in certain of its specific interpretations. Unfortunately, if organologists can see more instrumental detail in certain pictures than meets the naked eye, historians of musical thought are every bit as capable of attributing their own conceptions to the innocent citizens of an earlier age. A good example of deriving social music history from the

[19]See, for example, fig. 1 in the author's "Fifteenth Century Northern Book Painting."
[20]For two pioneer studies of the sort see Kathi Meyer-Baer, "Saints of Music," *Musica Disciplina* 9 (1955), 11-33; and Patricia Egan, "Poesia and the Fête Champêtre," *Art Bulletin* 41 (1959), 305-13.
[21]*Musikgeschichte in Bildern*, III/9 (Leipzig, 1976).
[22]*Die Musik der Engel* (Bern, 1962).

visual arts is the work of Richard Leppert, who has shown us a veritable world of seventeenth- and eighteenth-century bourgeois attitudes toward music.[23] All these examples, one notes, are characterized by a comparatively modest contribution of hard musicological data.[24]

Under this general rubric of social and intellectual history we can look at musical iconography in a still more radical way. Rather than study a large category of art with a view to reaching broad conclusions about the social or cultural history of music, one can focus upon a single picture or self-contained group of pictures for its own sake. That is to say a scholar can seek to reveal the meaning of some picture with musical subject matter for no other reason than that the picture is intriguing. This is musical iconography in the most proper sense. Iconography, after all, is simply that branch of art history which deals with the content of a picture rather than with its style. Musical iconography, in turn, is 'the study of the content of art works with musical subject matter. Accordingly, the musicological implications of the picture are incidental whether these implications are relevant to more conventional music historical questions, to musical thought, or whatever. The proper aim of the study is the picture itself, and its value lies in the inherent interest of the picture. There are as yet relatively few studies by musical iconographers which match this ideal, but among them there is one of classic execution—Tilman Seebass's book on early

[23]For two recent examples see "Concert in a House: Musical Iconography and Musical Thought," *Early Music* 7 (1979), 3-24; and "Johann Georg Plazer: Music and Visual Allegory," in *Music East and West: Essays in Honor of Walter Kaufmann*, ed. Thomas Noblitt (New York, 1981), pp. 209-24.

[24]Two recent studies by other authors which make good use of iconographic evidence in pursuit of what might be described as musical thought are: Barbara Russano Hanning, "Glorious Apollo: Poetic and Political Themes in the First Opera," *Renaissance Quarterly* 32 (1979), 485-513; and Claude V. Palisca, "G. B. Doni, Musicological Activist, and his 'Lyra Barberina'," *Modern Musical Scholarship*, pp. 180-205. A study which falls outside the categories proposed here, but which is too significant to ignore is Rebecca A. Baltzer's "Thirteenth-Century Illuminated Miniatures and the Date of the Florence Manuscript," *Journal of the American Musicological Society* 25 (1972), 1-18. The first half of the article is an interpretation of the manuscript's illustrations, a sound example of iconography in the proper sense; but the second half of the article, where it accomplishes its central aim of revising the manuscript's dates, uses artistic style rather than iconography.

medieval psalter illustration.[25] To be sure it makes a substantial contribution to organology in its exemplary study of early medieval instruments, and it affords us any number of valuable insights into early medieval musical thought, but certainly its central achievement is its altogether convincing explanation of the set of nine hitherto baffling illustrations of the Bibliothèque Nationale's ms *latin* 1118 tonary. The value of such study, then, lies not so much in its musicological implications as in the inherent interest of the art work involved and in the historical process whereby its origins are revealed.[26]

In thus closing this paper by singling out what might be called musical iconography in the pure sense, it is not my purpose to establish a hierarchy of value but only to suggest a measure of conceptual order. It is true that "pride of place" was assigned above to the social and intellectual history of music, but this is an observation based upon the nature of the artistic evidence, not a judgment on the superiority of one sort of study over the other. It remains a matter of choice whether one is to prefer, say, a substantial musicological result from viewing a large number of bad pictures or a purely iconographic result from one intriguing work of art. And then, too, such absolute separation seldom exists in practice; the best music iconographic studies, as we see in the case of Seebass, frequently yield a variety of results. But still there is one strong suggestion to be made here, and it is that the music iconographer must first come to terms with the work of art itself and only then turn to the evidentiary byproducts of the subject—whether they have to do with organology, performance practice, musical thought, or whether they exist at all.

---

[25] *Musikdarstellung und Psalterillustration im frühen Mittelalter* (Berlin, 1973).
[26] I tend to include within this category the excellent study of Colin Slim, "Mary Magdalene, Musician and Dancer," *Early Music* 8 (1980), 460-73. The author, however, in his response to the spoken version of this paper, which included a reference to his article, indicated disappointment in my failure to discuss the musical inscription of the Magdalene picture in question and indeed to mention musical inscriptions at all.

Musicology II

THE MUSICOLOGIST
TODAY AND IN THE FUTURE

Editor's Introduction

The American Musicological Society's 1981 Program Committee, acting on a suggestion from Claude Palisca, had the notion that sessions on the state of the discipline ought somehow to contrast the views of our established senior members with those of a newer generation. It was eventually decided to attempt this in two separate sessions.

The second session on American musicology was conceived with the premise that the third generation of American musicologists faces a variety of issues and problems unknown (or at least not applicable) to the founding fathers of the AMS and their original pupils. As our generation inherits, in some sense, responsibility for the discipline, these issues become ever more vital concerns, and concerns to be addressed in public forum. And so it was agreed to invite four "younger" musicologists—we used the term with due caution—to identify and discuss these issues in the light of their own experience in the profession.

In preliminary discussion and correspondence, the participants agreed to address four topics: the growing and complex relationship between musicologists and performers; the variety of institutional conditions under which we are expected to teach the history of music; questions of academic and non-academic publication of the results of scholarly inquiry; and the emerging discipline of music criticism. Richard Taruskin blushes with immodesty that his paper is a vindication of his own musical activity, but in fact each contribution has significant autobiographical components—as is only natural in seminars of this sort. A certain number of our beliefs are iconoclastic, and in some respects our panel may have ended up by involving itself with consciousness raising and subtle claiming of turf. But the panel clearly reflected (as a live event) and reflects (in written form) the evolving interests of today's younger scholars.

The discussion of the individual papers in Boston, where time allowed, was both collegial and vigorous. Taruskin was challenged by a Verdist for his skeptical remarks on historical reconstruction; the chairman tried to mediate this dispute by arguing for such reconstructionist performance on the ground of curiosity alone (though without questioning Taruskin's basic point that scholarship is necessary but insufficient for convincing performance). My own sense of scholarly "mission" was described by a colleague as naive (as though I were trying to proclaim some sort of *Neues-Davidsbund*); the counterargument here was that mission in itself is neither unscholarly nor unsophisticated, and it at least provides us with some rationale for what we do. Few of our number, though, seemed interested in arguing against the notion that scholarly publishing has tended to become both narrow-minded and uncomfortably tied up with questions of academic advancement. There was general agreement with and enthusiasm for Anne Hallmark's advocacy of underlying methodologic constancy in our teaching of historical issues. Rose Subotnik's impassioned and somewhat flamboyant apostrophe to free speech was met with what can only be termed shocked awe, as well as with considerable applause.

All four authors took the opportunity to revise their remarks and to add appropriate citations and references. Taruskin's article has been published in the *Journal of Musicology* (I/3, July 1982).

—**D. Kern Holoman**

A version of the following paper appears in *Journal of Musicology* I/3 (1982). Used by permission.

The Musicologist and the Performer

Richard Taruskin

The title of this panel may suggest that I will give a state-of-the-art report on the relationship between performance and musicology or else outline a program for the future development of that relationship. But neither would be worth my while to prepare or yours to listen to. Things

Richard Taruskin is Associate Professor of Music at Columbia University. His contribution to this symposium is closely related to his work as director of the early music ensemble, Cappella Nova. Additionally, Taruskin is a gambist and widely published writer on a variety of topics. He has been the recipient of both the Alfred Einstein and Noah Greenberg Awards of the American Musicological Society, the former for an article entitled "Opera and Drama in Russia: The Case of Serov's *Judith*," *Journal of the American Musicological Society* 32 (1979), 74-177; and the latter for a recording of Ockeghem's music (Musical Heritage Society 4026).

are going very well all by themselves. Never, it seems, have scholars and performers worked so closely and happily together or learned more from each other, nor have so many ever before combined the roles as successfully as now. Musicologically trained performers are proliferating in graduate programs around the country. Historical performance practice is now a recognized sub-discipline both of academic musicology and of conservatory curricula. When Mr. Henahan of the *New York Times* can devote a Sunday column to the merits of historical instruments, or when Mr. Rockwell of the same paper, in a glowing review of Pomerium Musices, can actually list among the group's assets that its director is a musicologist, we can all feel forgivably elated at going at last off the defensive *vis-à-vis* the public and the press. Let this trend of recognition continue. We've all worked hard for it and we deserve it, and everything I say here today is meant to abet it.

But at the same time I should like—among friends, as it were—to examine what Charles Rosen has recently called the "peculiar metaphysical and ontological assumptions"[1] that underly much current thinking about musicology and performance, or musicology-*cum*-performance, or even musicology versus performance. And if much of what follows sounds like an *apologia pro vita sua,* and therefore immodest, it is because I feel that the only way for me, as a musicologist-performer, to approach honestly the question of musicology and performance, is to look within.

So let me choose as my point of departure a little colloquy I had some time ago with a graduate student at Columbia, who undertook to tell me what was wrong with Cappella Nova, the Renaissance choral group I direct. He claimed that our performances were arbitrary and overly personal, and that I would be better advised to "let the music speak for itself." Well I can tell you that that rankled in its implication of irresponsibility. I do my homework, after all: I edit the music from its original sources, or at least from pedigreed *Gesamtausgaben;* I have read up on *musica ficta,* on text underlay, on proportions; we don't

---

[1]Charles Rosen, "The Musicological Marvel" (a review of *The New Grove*), *New York Review of Books* (28 May 1981), p. 36.

gussy up the music with instruments—and yet I knew just what the fellow meant and also that his view of our work was widely shared among scholars, or at least among graduate students. Debating the matter with him did me good. It made me examine my own premises with greater detachment than before, and made me attempt to separate my own musicological attitudes from my attitudes as a performer—something I rarely do consciously, any more than I am separately aware of inhaling and exhaling.

It seems a curious request to make of a performer, to "let the music speak for itself." If a performer did not have the urge to participate in it and, yes, to contribute to it, why then he wouldn't have become a performer in the first place. The only time I could recall being told previously to "let the music speak for itself" was when I played the opening movement of a Bach French Suite for my piano teacher many years ago and ventured a few ornaments. Most of the time the idea of letting the music speak for itself implies hostility, contempt, or at least mistrust of performers. It is what Brahms had in mind, for example, when he declined an invitation to the opera saying that if he sat at home with the score he'd hear a better performance. Or think of Stravinsky, with all his raillery against interpretation. Or Milton Babbitt, when describing his motives for adopting electronic media as a way of compensating for what he called the "low redundancy" of his music.[2]

All three composers share a view of performers as undesirable middle men, whose disappearance would enhance communication between composer and audience. But only in Babbitt's case was letting the music speak for itself a practicable alternative. Stravinsky, for his part, was moved by his mistrust of performers to become one himself, so as to document his music first in piano rolls and then in recordings and thus achieve the inviolable musical "object" he sought. The only trouble was that whenever Stravinsky documented his performance more than once he created quite different objects, particularly as regards tempo, which was always the main object of documentation to begin with. Moreover,

[2]Cf. "Who Cares if You Listen?" *High Fidelity,* vol. VIII, no. 2 (February 1958) and widely anthologized thereafter, e. g., in *Contemporary Composers on Contemporary Music,* ed. Elliott Schwartz and Barney Childs (New York, 1967; reprt. New York, 1978), pp. 244-50.

Stravinsky's recorded tempi were almost always faster than his indication in the score, sometimes by a truly bewildering margin, as in the case of *Zvezdoliki,* which I single out because Stravinsky referred to his recording of that piece in one of his conversation books as a particularly successful documentation.[3] So Stravinsky, sitting at home with the score like Brahms, heard a performance that was if not better, then at least consistently slower than the one he himself produced in actual sound. His efforts at documentation have only produced a confusing problem for those who would obey his wishes. But the problems he created are as nothing next to those created by such pianist-composers as Debussy or Prokofiev, whose recorded performances are so wildly at variance with their notation that no one could get away with copying them (as I found out when I took a Gavotte by Prokofiev to another piano teacher). As for Brahms himself, even if we allow that his remark àmounted to no more than persiflage, we may ask nonetheless whether the better performance he heard was better because it was more faithful to the music in some obscure way, or because it perfectly matched his tastes as another's rendition could not?

In short, music can never under any circumstances other than electronic speak for itself. In the case of notated music there is always a middle man, even if it is only ourselves as we contemplate the written symbols. And if anyone still doubts this let him drop in on any analysis symposium.

But let us assume that even if impossible to realize absolutely, "letting the music speak for itself" is still a worthy ideal to aspire to. What does it mean? For the moment let us assume it means realizing the composer's intentions as far as our knowledge of them permits. What we are really being told, then, is to "let the composer speak for himself." I will not rehearse here the familiar epistemological impediments to learning what the composer's intentions were, especially a composer as remote from us as Ockeghem, whose music I was enjoined to let speak for itself. I wish to go a bit further and suggest that in many if not most instances composers do not even have the intentions we would like to ascertain. And I am not

---

[3]"Contemporary Music and Recording," in Igor Stravinsky and Robert Craft, *Dialogues and a Diary* (Garden City, 1963), p. 33; also reprt. in Schwartz and Childs, p. 56.

even talking about what are sometimes called "high level" vs. "low level" intentions, that is, specific intentions with regard to individual pieces as opposed to assumptions based on prevailing conditions the composer took for granted.[4] No, I mean something even more fundamental: that composers' concerns are different from performers' concerns, and that once the piece is finished, the composer regards it and relates to it either as a performer, if he is one, or simply as a listener.

I'll give a few examples. One is Irving Berlin, who said of Fred Astaire, "I like him because he doesn't change my songs, or if he does, he makes them better." Another is Debussy again. He said to George Copeland on their first meeting that he never thought he'd hear his piano music played so well during his lifetime. No question then that Copeland's playing realized the composer's intentions to the latter's satisfaction. On another occasion, though, Debussy asked Copeland why he played the opening of *Reflets dans l'eau* the way he did. Copeland's response was that old performer's standby, calculated to make any musicologist see red: "Because I feel it that way." To which Debussy replied that as for himself he felt it differently, but that Copeland must go on playing it as he, Copeland, felt it.[5] So once the pianist's credentials as a Debussy performer were established, his performances were accepted by the composer as being no less authoritative than his own. Debussy, as pianist, was in his own eyes only one interpeter among others.

My next example stems from personal experience. I once sat in as page-turner at a rehearsal of Elliott Carter's *Duo* for violin and piano under the composer's supervision. He couldn't have been less helpful. Whenever the performers sought guidance on matters of balance or tempo, his reply was invariably, "I don't know; let's see," and then he would join them in seeking solutions, as often asking their advice as they his. At one point, when the performers where having some difficulty with his very finicky rhythmic notation, Carter said (so help me), "For

[4]Cf. Randall R. Dipert, "The Composer's Intentions: An Examination of their Relevance for Performance," *Musical Quarterly* 66 (1980), 205-18.
[5]Cf. George Copeland, "The First—and Last—Times I Saw Debussy," *Music*, preview issue (November 1844), pp. 6-9.

heaven's sake don't count—just feel it." At the end of the rehearsal he commented that every performance of the *Duo* was very different from every other one, but that "whichever one I'm hearing always seems the best." So much for intentions. If that was Carter's attitude, what do you suppose Ockeghem would have cared about Cappella Nova's ficta? We seem to be committing another "intentional fallacy" here, trying, just as Wimsatt and Beardsley said we should never do, to solve our problems by "consulting the oracle."[6]

It seems to me that much of what I will make bold to characterize as the "musicological" attitude toward performance is based on consulting the oracle in an even more spurious, because roundabout, way. We tend to assume that if we can recreate all the external conditions that obtained in the original performance of a piece we will thus recreate the composer's inner experience of the piece and thus allow him to speak for himself. In a lecture I recently attended on the staging of one of Verdi's operas in Paris, a great deal of fascinating detail was recounted on all the vicissitudes encountered in the course of mounting the work and in making it conform to the special demands of the Paris Opéra. The point was constantly reiterated that every aspect of the production was completely documented in surviving records, so that one could revive the work tomorrow just as it was being described. I ventured to ask at the end of the lecture why this would be desirable, and I was told, with eyebrows raised and voice high to show how obvious the answer was, that in this way the composer's intentions would be realized. And this after a lecture in which it had just been demonstrated that the intentions realized in the original production had belonged to many, not just Verdi, and that in a large number of instances the composer's intentions had been overruled and frustrated.

So why *do* we consult the oracle? A simple answer, the usual answer, is that we want our performances to be authentic. But that is no answer. What *is* this thing called authenticity, and why do we want it? While most of us would by now agree with the premise, so elegantly and humorously set forth by Michael Morrow in *Early Music* a few years

[6]W. K. Wimsatt, Jr., and Monroe C. Beardsley, "The Intentional Fallacy," *Sewanee Review* (1946), pp. 468-88.

ago,[7] that authenticity of the kind we usually have in mind when talking musicologically about performance practice is a chimera, most of us are nevertheless no more deterred by this realization from seeking it than was Bellérophon. Again I ask, why?

We usually trace the origins of modern musicology to romantic historicism. But it seems to me that musicological ideals of performance style owe as much if not more to the modernist aesthetic that rose to dominance out of the ashes of the first world war. We in music usually think of it as the Stravinskian aesthetic, though it had been anticipated with astonishing, if cranky, completeness as early as Hanslick's *The Beautiful in Music*. It is usually described, after Ortega y Gasset, as "dehumanization,"[8] but since that word (though meant by Ortega with approval) carries such unpleasant overtones, I prefer to use T. S. Eliot's term, depersonalization, defined as "the surrender of [the artist] as he is at the moment to something much more valuable," that thing being Tradition, which, as Eliot warns us, "cannot be inherited, and if you want it you must obtain it by great labour."[9] And why do we want it? So that our performances may capture something of what the folklorist Jeffrey Mark so percipiently described half a century ago in an article entitled "The Fundamental Qualities of Folk Music," but which is

[7] Michael Morrow, "Musical Performance and Authenticity," *Early Music* 6 (1978), 233-46.

[8] Cf. José Ortega y Gasset, "The Dehumanization of Art," in *The Dehumanization of Art and Other Essays on Art, Culture, and Literature* (Princeton, 1968), pp. 3-56.

[9] "Tradition and the Individual Talent," in *Selected Prose of T. S. Eliot*, ed. Frank Kermode (New York, 1975), pp. 40, 38. Of course the modernist and historicist positions are in many ways congruent and to a considerable degree symbiotic in their influence on musicological attitudes toward performance. Were it not for the historicist precept, instilled in all traditionally trained historians today, that one's contemporary attitudes and values must be suspended when confronting the past, it is doubtful whether "authentic performance" would have become the musicological issue it has, or whether in fact there would have been much impetus toward the practical revival of old performance practices to begin with. But without the support of the modernist philosophy examined here, it is just as doubtful whether the "Aufführungspraxis" movement would have achieved much resonance beyond the classroom and the Collegium Musicum. The thriving existence of *Early Music* magazine is in its paradoxical way the best testimony to the continued vitality of aesthetic modernism. The "early music boom" represents the precise locus of the confluence of historicism and modernism in music.

actually the best characterization I know of the modernist aesthetic as applied to music:

> The performer, whether as singer, dancer, or player, does his part without giving any or much impression that he is participating in the act. And his native wood notes wild, far from giving the popularly conceived effect of a free and careless improvisation, show him definitely to be in the grip of a remorseless and comparatively inelastic tradition which gives him little or no scope for personal expression (again as popularly conceived). *Through him the culture speaks,* and he has neither the desire nor the specific comprehension to mutilate what he has received. His whole attitude and manner [is] one of profound gravity and cool, inevitable intention. There [is] not the faintest suggestion of the flushed cheek and the sparkling eye. And [the performance] is ten times the more impressive because of it.[10]

So here at last is the real challenge issued by my critic in the encounter I began by describing: "Let the culture speak for itself." Ah, would that we could, for this is what genuine authenticity is, the kind Eliot wrote about, not what Michael Morrow called the "contemporary cult meaning" of the word, which is really just time-travel nostalgia. The trouble is that the artifacts of past culture with which Eliot dealt are still intact and available in a way that musical artifacts obviously can never be. Music has to be imaginatively recreated in order to be retrieved, and here is where conflicts are likely to arise between the performer's imagination and the scholar's conscience, even (or especially) when the two are housed in a single mind.

Verdi, speaking ironically about the aims of *verismo,* said: "It's fine to reproduce reality, but how much better to create it." I would paraphrase this to read: "It's fine to assemble the shards of a lost performance tradition, but how much better to reinvent it." Research alone has never given, and is never likely to give (again for obvious reasons) enough information to achieve that wholeness of conception and that sureness of style—in a word, that fearlessness—any authentic, which is to say,

[10]Jeffrey Mark, "The Fundamental Qualities of Folk Music," *Music and Letters* 10 (1929), 287-90 *passim.* Italics added.

authoritative, performance must embody. Here is a paradox: which is more "authentic," an historical reconstructionist performance of, say, *Messiah,* or a Three Choirs Festival performance? Which, in other words, enjoys the commonality of work, performer, and (lest we forget) audience, the certainty of experience and of expectation that lends the proceedings the "cool, inevitable intention" Jeffrey Mark described? The Three Choirs performance certainly speaks for a culture, not Handel's perhaps, but that of the performers and their audience certainly. It gives what Eliot called a sense "not only of the pastness of the past, but its presence."[11] The modernist, avant-garde, historical reconstruction of *Messiah* can only evoke the pastness of the past, and will therefore appeal not to the aesthetic sense but merely to antiquarian curiosity—unless it derives its sustenance not only from whatever evidence musicological research may provide, but from imaginative leaps that will fill in the gaps research by its very nature must leave. Otherwise we will have not a performance but a documentation of the state of knowledge. As long as the reconstructionist performer holds himself to the same strict standards of accountability we rightly demand of any scholar, his efforts will be bent not on doing what the music was meant to do, but on simply "getting it right," that is, on achieving what the mainstream performer takes for granted. He will end up, if he is lucky, with what the mainstream performer starts out with.

The most authoritative and convincing reconstructionist performances of early music, as well as the most controversial, have always been those that have proceeded from a vividly imagined—that is to say, frankly imaginary—but coherent performance style. They provide themselves with Tradition, in the Eliot sense, and bestow authenticity upon themselves. Where such performers do not know the composer's intentions they are unafraid to have intentions of their own, and to treat them with a comparable respect. I suppose I am thinking now of the performances of the Early Music Quartet and some recent ones by the Concentus Musicus among those I have heard, and among those I have not, of the radical reconstructionist performance ·of *Messiah* given in Ann Arbor under Edward Parmentier a year ago,

[11]Eliot, p. 38.

which I know only by enthusiastic rumor, and by reports of the uproar it created among some of the scholars in attendance.

In this light, let me return now to the criticisms of Cappella Nova. What was mainly under attack was our approach to phrasing and dynamics, both of which are very sharply profiled in our performances, and which from the very beginning have always been singled out by our hearers either for praise or for blame. The origins of the approach lie, I have no hesitation in admitting, in my own subjective response to the nature of the lines in complex, melismatic, and polyphonic textures. I know of no specific historical sanction for it, except insofar as subjective responses of contemporary hearers have been occasionally and vaguely recorded. In the absence of hard evidence I have felt not only free but duty bound to invent an approach. Or, to put things as they really happened, it was because this approach to phrasing and dynamics evolved in me during my period as director of the Columbia Collegium Musicum, that I felt I had a statement to make about the music and was moved to form the group in the first place. Although its origins lay not in certain knowledge but in imagination, the approach is very much an objective feature of Cappella Nova's style. It is an element of what we take to be and present as the authentic sound of the music, and its presence is, far from an intrusion, quite necessary if for us the music is, yes, to "speak for itself." Those whose scholar's conscience equates silence with prohibition must inevitably regard our performances as arbitrary, but really arbitrary in my view are the flat dynamics and the lack of phrasing, that is, of molding lines to their highpoints, which characterize many so-called "objective" performances of Renaissance music. For these derive not from any condition or feature of the music or of its historical context, but merely from the state of evidence, over which the performer can exercise no control. Strict accountability thus reduces performance practice to a lottery. It doesn't have anything to do with authenticity. Authenticity stems from conviction. Conviction, in turn, stems as much from belief as it does from knowledge. Our beliefs—naive or sophisticated, to be sure, depending on the state of our knowledge—are what can give us the sense of assurance possessed by those fortunate enough to have behind them an unbroken tradition of performance.

This brings me to a perhaps even more fundamental caveat. What, after all, is historical method, and to what kind of knowledge does it lead? If we were to reduce it all to a single word, that word would have to be generalization. Style criticism, often held up as the ultimate goal of historical scholarship in music, is above all the abstraction of contexts from cases, the establishment of generalizing criteria. Think of Riemann, for example, of whom we read in *The New Grove* that "he was not interested in the individual case as such, but rather in discerning its typicality and its place in the entire system."[12] And, of course, most properly historical musicological work is either that or it is a preparation for that. But this is as far from the performer's mentality as it is possible to be. *His* concern is only with the individual case, taken one at a time. As George Perle remarked admiringly about Seiji Ozawa, who was performing one of his works at Tanglewood, "When he's playing it his whole repertoire consists of one piece—mine." And here is what Erich Leinsdorf has to say in a recent book which was actually meant as a polemic against interpretive excess: "Every great work is first and last a meaningful musical utterance unlike any other. If it did not have its own unique meaning it would have come and gone and would not be part of our living repertoire."[13] Leinsdorf's words are fighting words, and what he is fighting is what he calls the "sacrifice of the sense of music to a simplistic notion of period style." For him, then, historical reconstruction is just another variety of interpretive excess. But one needn't accept his belligerent equation of style consciousness with simplemindedness to note the real enough danger of our sense of style becoming reductive, owing to an insufficient appreciation of or response to the uniqueness of individual compositions.

[12]Mark Hoffman, article "Riemann, Hugo," in *The New Grove Dictionary of Music and Musicians* (London, 1980), XVI, 5.
[13]Erich Leinsdorf, *The Composer's Advocate: A Radical Orthodoxy for Musicians* (New Haven, 1981), 88-89.

This is a very easy trap to fall into. Our training as scholars gives us very precise and efficient ways of dealing with generalities. We have a vocabulary for them, and the process of framing them invokes reassuringly scientific methods and criteria, many of them quantitative and exact. We have no such aids in dealing with uniqueness. We have no vocabulary: words can no more give an exact representation of an individual piece of music than they can render an individual face. We have to draw the face and play the piece. But nothing makes a scholar more insecure than being at a loss for words. And nothing is less scientific than the evaluation not of quantities but of artistic qualities, the specific details, the "divine details," as Nabokov would say. These must be apprehended by imaginative response, empathic identification, artistic insight—all euphemisms, of course, for intuition, which word embarrasses and antagonizes the scholar in us. Unwilling to claim intuition as a guide, both for the reason just given and for the reason given a while ago—that it violates our scholarly principles of accountability—we often tend to flee from characterizing the uniqueness of a piece in performance, and seek our refuge in our objective knowledge, which is in all cases a generalized one. Since it is never possible to talk about the unique with the same objectivity as one can about the typical, we are tempted to ignore distinguishing characteristics and instead parade our basic knowledge of style as if it were specific insight. The results are familiar, typified, if you will, by performances of choral masterpieces by Bach or Handel that reduce them to demonstrations of dance tempi, A-415, and (*pace* Professor Neumann!) *notes inégales.*

There is a corollary to this in the form of reliance upon authentic editions, authentic instruments, or authentic performance practices learned from authentic treatises in place of careful and independent consideration of the music. An actual, if extreme, recent example was an advertising flyer sent out by a New York harpsichordist announcing that his would be the first New York performance of the Goldberg Variations from the *Neue Bach Ausgabe.* This kind of thing is the performer's analogue to what is regrettably becoming a pair of recognizable types among scholarly papers—the kind that merely lists variants between versions or sources, and the kind that makes an exhaustive physical description of a sketch, both kinds purporting meanwhile to describe "compositional process." This is preparatory work offered as the substance of scholarship. Similarly a performance that merely sets out to demonstrate that Bach was Baroque represents preparatory work, not the substance of performance.

But even at their best and most successful, or especially at their best and most successful, historical reconstructionist performances are in no sense recreations of the past. They are quintessentially modern performances, modernist performances in fact, the product of an aesthetic wholly of our own era, no less time-bound than the performance styles they would supplant. Like all other modernist philosophies, historical reconstructionism views the work of art, including performing art, as an autonomous object, not as a process, not as an activity. It views the internal relationships of an art work as synonymous with its content, and in the case of music it renounces all distinction between sound and substance: to realize the sound is in fact to realize the substance, hence the enormous and, be it said, oft-times exaggerated concern today for the use of authentic period instruments for all periods. The aim of historical reconstruction is, as Ortega put it, "a scrupulous realization,"[14] and as Eliot put it, "not a turning loose of emotion, but an escape from emotion; . . . not the expression of personality, but an escape from personality,"[15] the emotions and the personality escaped from being, of course, those of the performer "as he is at the moment."[16] The artist trades in objective, factual knowledge,

[14]"The Dehumanization of Art," p. 14.
[15]"Tradition and the Individual Talent," p. 43.
[16]The invention of sound recording has obviously been a tremendous spur to this tendency, since it offers the possibility of permanence to a medium that had formerly existed only "at the moment." Most historical reconstructionist performance aspires at least tacitly to the status of document, if not that of *Denkmal*. When the performance is recorded, the aim usually becomes explicit (witness the slogan of the SEON series of historical recordings: "Document & Masterwork"). No less than the score, the performance is regarded as a "text" rather than as an activity, and this creates another pressure toward the elimination from it of anything spontaneous or "merely" personal, let alone idiosyncratic.

not subjective feelings. His aim is not direct communication with his audience but something he sees as a much higher, in Eliot's words, "much more valuable" goal, communion with Art itself and with its history, and he enlists musicology's aid in achieving it.

To return once more to the starting point, this is what is meant today by "letting the music speak for itself." I am describing no monstrosity, no straw man, but an ideal of beauty that inspired many of the greatest creative minds of our century. And it is only in the nature of things that what dominated advanced recreative minds half a century ago should be dominating advanced recreative minds today. The paradox and the problem—or is it just my problem?—is that this way of thinking about art and performance has no demonstrable relevance to the ways people thought about art and performance before the twentieth century. Applied to the music of the Renaissance and the Baroque, to say nothing of the nineteenth century, it all seems exquisitely anachronistic. And what seems to prove my point is that with the possible exception of the rather ambiguous case of continuo realization, the modern reconstructionist movement has produced many scrupulous realizers of musical notation but has yet to produce a single genuine master of improvisation, which we all know to have been nine-tenths of the Renaissance and Baroque musical icebergs.

Some may be wondering now who I'm really thinking of. But I am thinking of no individual; I am thinking of a little bit of each of us. We all share these attitudes to some extent if we are at all alive to our own time. Do I seem then to be generally skeptical of historical reconstructionism or of musicology as an ally of performance? Nothing could be further from the truth, as I hope my own activities testify. But I am skeptical of the complacency with which difficult issues are often addressed, and I do deplore the equation of modernist objectivity with scientific truth. Having used the word, I feel I must say a thing or two about "scientific" attitudes, though I fear these remarks will be the most controversial of all. Empirical science, as all the world knows, claims to be "value-free." But art is not, and performance must not be. The adoption of the doctrinaire empiricist, positivist stance of scientific research when investigating performance practice can be pernicious, leading in extreme cases to an evasion of responsibility, something distressingly close to a musical Eichmann defense. I have in mind the perpetration of musical results that the performer himself regards as unattractive, in the the belief that that's how it was done, like it or not ("I was just following orders"). There have been notable recent instances of this in Bach performance, where the situation is exacerbated by the knowledge that Bach himself did not like certain aspects of his own performance practice, notably involving the size and quality of his choir in Leipzig. Still more disturbing is the "scientific" pressure to keep up with the state of research, whatever one's personal predilections. I know of more than one instance in which performers of Renaissance and Baroque music have followed practices of which they were not personally convinced either historically or aesthetically for fear that otherwise they might be suspected of ignorance.

To even the score now, and to return to a more personal note, let me attempt to list the assets my musicological training has given me as a performer. At the very top of the list goes curiosity, with its implications, so far as human nature allows, of openmindedness, receptivity to new ideas, and love of experiment. It is in this spirit that I believe investigations of past performance practices should be conducted. Let us indeed try out everything we may learn about in every treatise, every archival document, every picture, every literary description, and the more adventurously the better. But let us not do it in a spirit of dutiful self-denial or with illusions that the more knowledge one garners, the fewer decisions one will have to make. Let us accept from the scholar in us only that which genuinely excites the performer in us, if for no other reason than because both the attractive and the unattractive finding are equally likely to be wrong. Above all, let us not be afraid, as Rose Subotnik puts it with respect to criticism, to "acknowledge our own presence" in our work and to accept it, if for no other reason than because it is in the final analysis inescapable. The suspension of personality in a modernist performance immediately stamps the performance as such, and is paradoxically tantamount to an assertion of personality. We impose our aesthetic on Bach no less than did Liszt, Busoni, or Stokowski.

The second great advantage musicological training confers is knowledge of what there is and where and how to get at it. When one has mastered a scholar's bibliographical and paleographical skills, one need not be limited by the vagaries of editors and publishers. But here too there is an attendant pitfall in the form of an overly bibliographical approach to programming. I have in mind the kind of program that starts off with sixteen settings of *J'ay pris amours,* followed by one *bassadanza* from each of five collections, and finally a Machaut chanson performed with two voices, then three voices, then four voices as it is transmitted in three different sources. These are seminar papers in sound, not concert programs. And another didactic programming pitfall is the practice, once far more widespread than it is now (as those who attended the Josquin Festival-Conference ten years ago may recall)[17] of presenting a kind of analysis of a piece in lieu of a performance of it—for example, changing the scoring of each *talea* of an isorhythmic motet, or bringing out by hook or crook the cantus firmus of any mass or motet. In either event, the performer takes it upon himself to throw into relief something the composer in many cases took pains to conceal, and is being the very opposite of authentic, however you construe the word. We tend, many of us, particularly those of us who teach music history for our daily bread, to turn our concerts into classrooms, and I know from personal experience that no bad performer's habit born of musicology is more difficult to break. It is a case of the scholar's conscience once more, this time actually masquerading as the performer's imagination.

Speaking of teaching and of classrooms reminds me that when thinking of the relationship between the musicologist and the performer we usually assume that the former teaches and the latter learns. But good performers can teach receptive scholars a great deal, and communication both ways is needed if a real symbiosis of musicology

[17]See the transcripts of the "Workshop on Performance and Interpretation" published along with the rest of the proceedings of the Festival-Conference in *Josquin des Prez,* ed. Edward E. Lowinsky with the collaboration of Bonnie J. Blackburn (London, 1976), pp. 645-719, and most especially, Ludwig Finscher's paper, "Historical Reconstruction Versus Structural Interpretation in the Performance of Josquin's Motets" in the same volume, pp. 627-32.

and performance is to occur. Sometimes one is lucky enough to have it happen within oneself if one combines the roles. It was the performer in me that taught the scholar in me the extent to which *modus*, though not explicit in the notation, continues to operate throughout the Renaissance period, at least in church music, as an organizer of rhythm. This is a feature totally obscured by modern editions which base their barring on the *tactus*—a feature of modern editorial practice which, as Lowinsky demonstrated over twenty years ago,[18] is perfectly authentic, but, for a final paradox, none the less a falsification. For *modus* is, as I have come to believe, the operative factor in projecting the rhythmic life of much of Isaac, for example, or of Josquin. It is a matter I intend to pursue in the context of "pure research," but it was a discovery I made purely serendipitously as a performer.

I began this little talk by noting that musicologists and performers are on better terms now than ever before, and I wish to reaffirm this heartening fact in conclusion. It might not be amiss to recall that it was not always so. Dmitri Shostakovich once had a good laugh over a definition of a musicologist he heard at breakfast one day from his piano teacher, and repeated it all his life. "What's a musicologist? I'll tell you. Our cook, Pasha, prepared the scrambled eggs for us, and we are eating them. Now imagine a person who did not cook the eggs and does not eat them, but talks about them—that is a musicologist."[19] Well, we're eating them now, and even cook up a few on occasion, as when we do a little discreet composing to make a fragmentary piece performable. Now, if we could only sell them . . .

---

[18]Lowinsky, "Early Scores in Manuscript," *Journal of the American Musicological Society* 13 (1960), 126-73.
[19]Nikolai Malko, *A Certain Art* (New York, 1966), p. 180.

Publishing and/or Perishing

D. Kern Holoman

Unlike many of the essays in the present volume, the remarks in mine are rather more in the nature of practical advice than conceptual or philosophical discourse. That sentence is not meant as an apology, for surely much of what is said elsewhere in this little book is predicated on the notion that musicological exchange deserves a practical public forum, and surely the search for such a forum (and the disappointment when it cannot be found) is familiar to us all. Then, too, publishing practices have a direct bearing on the effect (I hesitate to say, the impact) our ideas have on other thinking people. Hugh Macdonald is

D. Kern Holoman is Professor and Chairman of Music at the University of California, Davis, where he conducts the University Symphony Orchestra. He is managing editor of the journal *19th-Century Music*.

fond of describing scholarly effort as either "interesting but unimportant," or "important but not interesting"; I would search for a musicology that avoids both pitfalls.

We might as well acknowledge, to start with, that the traditional, omni-directional alliance between the scholarly community and the world of book and journal publishing makes for a curious, though not altogether unwholesome, sort of academic incest. The scholar needs the publisher to disseminate the results of research; the publisher must publish in order to stay in business. The publisher provides standards (and, through his editorial board, an apparatus) for the assessment of scholarly merit; he does it by relying on the advice of writers themselves.[1] But alliance breeds reliance, and especially in a smallish discipline like musicology, there is some danger of creating a network of Old Boys and Girls. Later on I shall suggest that the situation is not so sinister after all; for the moment the point is that the chain of command can be confusing to the young writer seeking publication of his work.

Most musicologists are university-born and -bred, and there the published study is primary evidence of expertise and recognition. It is the evidence most frequently proffered for academic advancement—for, to put it bluntly, getting and keeping a job. That makes our stake in publication high, yet we might as well face up to one obvious result of such a system: the pages of our periodicals and our books are too frequently unappetizing. An even more alarming outgrowth of the system is that sooner or later many of us come perilously close to forming the conclusion that our research and writing, and the *de facto* obligation to keep filling blank pages, bear little relation to our professional obligations as teachers, performers, and administrators. This line of thought can lead to a queasy feeling that academic life, which we want to believe in as the good life, is incoherent and lacks a fulfilling sense of direction and program. Anne Hallmark's gloom ("jobs that require too much of us on too many different fronts; . . . our dreams must be shrunk") rings all too true. And so writing becomes a distasteful

---

[1]On these issues, see Willard A. Lockwood, "The Decision to Publish: Scholarly Standards," in *Scholars and their Publishers,* ed. Weldon A. Kefauver (New York: Modern Language Association of America, 1977), pp. 6-17.

task, which it ought never be. The scholar begins to write because he must write rather than because he has something he must say.

On top of these more-or-less traditional dilemmas, shared by scholars of all ages and disciplines, are some unique to our time and to our craft. The information explosion, about which Claude Palisca writes above, isn't just imaginary, and it is no joke. It gives us two new problems: merely coping with all we know (or can know, or should know), and dealing with the certainty that a newly found or recovered fact, however important, must compete for attention in a veritable fallout of facts generated by information-explosion technology. A lifetime seems short enough to master, say, the compositions of Beethoven; nowadays one feels a moral obligation to know, in addition, everything one can of sketchbooks, conversation books, metronomes, period pianos, and the work of Cherubini and Clementi. And at the same time, I share with my colleagues an abiding fear of the results of over-specialization and a yearning for the magisterial command of the musicologist-virtuosi—Abraham, Lang, Seeger, Strunk—of a simpler time.

We share, in fact, a variety of inflations. Not least of these is the inflated job requirement—inflated merely for the convenience of the employer. Then there is the inflated and artificial expectation for advancement: thus and such a number of articles, and the book well on its way, for tenure. More must be better. All this comes at a juncture in musicology when mastery of a field and development of a true and coherent program of research take, by necessity, longer and longer. And yet the earlier we find ourselves in our careers, the more we hear a message echoing all around us: publish, publish, publish. It has become part of the ethos of musicology.

But we all know that too much is written, especially by younger Americans. We (younger scholars, I mean) do not enjoy a particularly high reputation for our work, either nationally or internationally. One foreigner wrote (I paraphrase his remarks): "We are not all that well off for article material that is publishable; we get an awful lot of horrible stuff from Americans I have never heard of; I suppose the authors are all seeking tenure through publication, come what may; it seems a dreadful system to me." Some years before, Joseph Boonin wrote in a similar vein: "Much, perhaps too much, is written and published on music today."[2] Claire Brook, writing about how book manuscripts are acquired, concludes with the over-the-transom method, and she is not overly optimistic: "Finally, there are the inevitable revised dissertations, enlarged monographs, expanded articles, translations from the Sanskrit. Much of this may be academic detritus, to be sure, but from time to time, there may be a great 'find'."[3]

One reason for this widespread lack of enthusiasm for modern written musicology may be that we have come to think a written piece must somehow be *severe*. It must also, we seem to think, draw the attention of its readers to a minute new point and proclaim shattering implications of the point for our perception of some vital strand in the web of music history. This must be accomplished with a great show of scholarly apparatus, leaving no detail unmentioned or uncited. And as for citations, the scholarly essay must, of course, have many footnotes—for academic advancement is vulgarly thought to rest on tallies: of titles, words, and yes, of footnotes. If possible it should be, as we are fond of saying, *about the music;* this will offer opportunities for a *recherché* graph or two, and for several dozen musical examples. The essay should demonstrate at least method, and if possible, a *methodology*. And the longer the better, never mind that with all this inflation the number of minutes in the day has clearly shrunk.

No, what is surely the most important attribute of good writing—the kind publishers publish—is craft, discipline, and technique: in a word, style. It must grasp the fancy with the same qualities of structural coherence that we admire in musical composition; it should have convincing rhythm, tone quality, and pitch. It must, that is, exult in the language. Yet there can be no doubt that writing sensibly about music and music history is a tall order. Even when we are addressing each other and using our own vocabulary, describing what happens in our art is often a painful process. This situation, along with accompanying

[2]"Music Publishing Today—A Symposium," *Notes* 32 (1975), 223-58; Boonin's contribution appears on pp. 230-35, and the citation is from p. 231.
[3]"Music Publishing Today," p. 246; Mrs. Brook's remarks appear on pp. 243-48.

difficulties of translation, definition, and the like, seems to me to render craft decidedly more important in musicological prose than in other kinds of historical writing.

Good writing about music, in short, is seductive in the prose itself; it can even be memorable. It was Arthur Mendel who memorialized Cromwell for most of us: "I beseech you, in the bowels of Christ, think it possible you may be mistaken."[4] Edward T. Cone entitles two important articles "Inside the Saint's Head" and "Three Ways of Reading a Detective Story—or a Brahms Intermezzo,"[5] and in so doing forces on us the most difficult step of all, reading the first line. And who can forget those immortal words, "shabby little shocker"?

(Good writing does not necessarily make for easy reading. *The Classical Style* is a difficult read, and I, for one, would not hold it up as an example of a prose to imitate; nevertheless its stature as a powerful and influential piece of writing cannot be denied. I am merely arguing against needlessly contrived scholarly prose.)

What is worth saying is worth saying well. I dwell on this matter of style for two reasons. First, because we are fortunate enough to be heirs to a high tradition of American musicological prose; there is excellent work to study, admire, and imitate. Likewise, the literary value of American letters in this century, from Edmund Wilson on the one hand to E. B. White on the other, is a heritage of substantive worth. We should be quicker to perceive writing about music as literature, not just as a technique of getting things said; musicologists should cultivate literary style. A little Modern Language Association pamphlet, *The Publication of Academic Writing,* sums it up forthrightly: "What is said in a scholarly work is clearly of prime importance; but the way in which it is said is hardly less important."[6]

---

[4]"Evidence and Explanation," *International Musicological Society: Report of the Eighth Congress, New York, 1961,* vol. II (Kassel, 1962), pp. 3-18; the citation appears on p. 18.
[5]"Inside the Saint's Head," *Musical Newsletter* 1 (1971), 3-12, 16-20; and 2 (1972), 19-22; "Three Ways of Reading a Detective Story—or a Brahms Intermezzo," *Georgia Review* 31 (1977), 554-74.
[6]*The Publication of Academic Writing,* ed. Oscar Cargill, William Charvat, and Donald D. Walsh (New York: Modern Language Association of America, 1966), p. 7.

Finally, good writing is about important things. The more obscure the topic or the lesson, the more it will have to prove its worth. Skillful musicology, then, recognizes what Palisca calls "the point of diminishing relevance," and it recognizes, in turn, the timeless wonder of the greatest artists and their work. Contrary to notions held commonly in our graduate schools, there is no dearth of important issues to be faced nor of significant research to be done. There can never be: Bach, Beethoven, and Stravinsky research is hardly over, and their lives and work will inexorably attract the attention of many of our most gifted scholars. The results of lively scholarship are self-perpetuating. Who, for that matter, *is* to write the long-awaited synthesis of the New Bach Scholarship?

Cultivated written style and periodic recommitment to humane ideals for our work should go a long way toward improving the palatability of musicological writing. Some refinement in our conception of the publishing trade itself can make things better still. The following are practical issues, mostly about the mechanics of journalistic enterprise. They are raised here in the conviction that one reason editors and writers become adversaries, and unnecessarily so, is that the writer fails properly to envisage the situation at the other end.

Editorial altruism and high-mindedness is ever weighed against the cost of the enterprise. Production cost is measured in terms of money, time, and space, and there is never enough of any of it. Budgets (of money, time, and space) are fixed, as everybody knows, months in advance of the actual event of publication, with the result that the most common obstacle barring the decision to publish (and particularly the decision to publish in a timely fashion) is cost. Anything the writer can do to minimize the cost of his proposed venture is an argument in favor of publication.

An appropriate beginning is to master the rudiments of manuscript preparation. Two steps, simple though they be, are traditionally overlooked in authorial impatience to reach print; these are careful perusal of *A Manual of Style* (University of Chicago Press, 12th edn., 1969; better, the newly-issued 13th edn., 1982), on which nearly every publisher bases his house style, and adoption of the precepts set forth in any particular journal's Directions to Contributors. Then there are a number of good primers, including the symposium and two pamphlets already cited in this essay: "Music Publishers Today—A Symposium," in *Notes* 32 (1975), 223-58; *The Publication of Academic Writing;* and *Scholars and Their Publishers.* For those determined to understand the subtler mysteries of the trade, there is even a professional journal, *Scholarly Publishing.*

Now I propose a paradox: most submissions to editors and publishers are declined, yet those very editors and publishers are on constant, sometimes backbiting, lookout for material. A number of logical conclusions can be formed from this proposition, conclusions which require little further elaboration.

The first is that the editorial stance of a publication greatly affects the decision to publish. A manuscript should be nudged into a configuration commensurate with the spectrum of qualities for which the intended publication stands. A second corollary is that it is more difficult than authors apparently think to meet, at one and the same time, both the academic and the literary desiderata of most publishers—in short, that prevailing notions of stylish musicological prose strike editors as wrongheaded. An observation that follows from much of what I have said above is that brevity (or, better, concision) is much to be valued. A final conclusion is that much writing seems to those assessing it to lack focus on an appropriate, and an appropriately wide, readership. The question of audience is at the heart of the last section of my paper.

This is not an essay about the bewildering world of advanced, dare I say "state-of-the-art" technologies, with all their joys and their sorrows. Nevertheless, it seems reasonable to cite familiarity with modern techniques of book production as another potential way to speed publication. These techniques evolve only a shade less rapidly than missile technology and home video games, but they need not frighten, us, and—much though we all admire the look of traditional "hot" type—it is futile to imagine a return to the old ways. Broken type and inverted letters, then, are out; faulty paste-up, poor spacing of diacriticals, and hopeless word division are in. Perceptive readers of the modern daily press have been amusing themselves for some time by devising foolproof rules for computerized wordbreaks; the musicologist will wish to devise them such that they will explain to a machine how to divide that most difficult of words, "Beethoven."

A word, too, about economics. In days of yore, knight-musicologists in towers purported to be of ivory (or, at least, of ivy) could shun participatory economics; today's political and social awareness must be complemented with economic realism. There is a rule of thumb among publishers that if every poet were to buy one published book of poetry each year, the publishing of poetry would become economically viable.[7] With our lavish university and departmental libraries, our access to offprints, and above all our Xerox machines, it is tempting to forget to purchase books and journals for ourselves. Across the country you can hear university press representatives lamenting over how difficult it is to sell a thousand copies of anything. It should give us pause to note, then, that one-third the membership of the American Musicological Society (never mind all other practicing professional musicians and serious amateurs, nor the several hundred institutional subscribers listed at the close of the AMS directory) could guarantee a respectable sale.

Mrs. Brook puts it more strongly:

> [I] will now call upon the reader to pay *his* dues: *buy* the books of which you approve; do not limit your support to the ubiquitous "desk" copy. Recommend those books to your students and order them for your library. Complain to the publisher about slovenly typesetting and proofreading, shoddy and gimmicky "packages," illegible musical examples, imperfect binding, built-in obsolescence. Discourage the thoughtless and illegal use of the Xerox machine. . . . Above all, you, the

[7]See Herbert S. Bailey, Jr., "The Decision to Publish: Economic Factors," in *Scholars and Their Publishers*, pp. 18-26.

reader, must demand literary, as well as scholarly quality in all professional publications, regardless of price or provenance.[8]

We can only concur, and with the utmost vigor. The scholar's ultimate clout is his combination of brains and discriminating purse.

Reading through the present volume, I am struck by how often the same issues surface in radically differing guises and contexts. Clearly the most important of these, for it is mentioned in nearly every essay, is the need for musicology to be (or at least to seem) more important. It is behind Kerman's familiar advocacy of criticism and Taruskin's affection for the concert hall, behind Treitler's hope for a more expansive analysis and Hallmark's search for renewed philosophies of teaching. Palisca complained a decade ago of the isolation of musicology from the public and of "the alienation of lay music-lovers and general historians." "The music scholar," he writes, "tends to operate in the hermetic atmosphere of libraries, institutes, and seminars and to communicate through specialized reviews. Few of his discoveries and interpretations leak out to the general public."

What it seems to me all of us are advocating, each in his own way, is scholarly activism. Published musicology should be a more vital force in American culture and American letters than it is.

Musicology, however defined and delimited, advocates erudition and rigor of method. Taruskin calls its primary attribute "curiosity: [i.e.,] openmindedness, receptivity to new ideas, and love of experiment." Activist musicology retains the erudition and the rigor; it values curiosity above all. And additionally, it values itself enough to imagine that men of letters in all walks of life should profit from it, and that it should profit from them. It has, in short, a mission, one which has something to do with keeping alive the ideals of functional literacy in the arts.

It is a battle wageable, and to be waged on all fronts. Activist musicology would not deny either the importance of "popularizing"

[8]"Music Publishing Today," pp. 247-48.

efforts or professional stature to those who practice them. More musicologists than ever are finding gainful and rewarding work in the media, with opera and orchestra associations, and now in the extraordinary new world of cable-conveyed video and information.[9] These are good and exciting things, for they can bring the attitudes and accomplishments of musicology to a wide public. They need only be complemented by a return to musicological activism in the writing of general works for the book-buying public. In Michael Steinberg's words, "The opportunity to help people find a way into a difficult musical experience—perhaps intrinsically and permanently difficult, perhaps difficult only because of unfamiliarity—is more than an opportunity. It is an obligation."[10]

To return to the strange bedfellows with which our essay opened: the enterprises of publication and musicology need be symbiotic and not parasitic. Put another way, "scholars are not standing on the outside of the publication system looking in; they are on both sides of the equation."[11] If for no other reason than that we are musicians (and therefore artists, and therefore practitioners of perhaps the highest of callings), we must consciously strive for what I have called loftiness of purpose in our own writing, for it is only in so doing that we can discover Palisca's "yardsticks of relevance." Need it be said that as evaluators of our colleagues, particularly at the campus level, we must set as a measure of excellence broad recognition of expertise over tallies of things?

Our professional societies must welcome these changes: toward new fields, new audiences, and a new flexibility. They must welcome these changes by abandoning traditional and prejudicial notions of the "appropriate" modes of expression. For musicology, properly

[9]See the report on the session "Music and the Mass Media," in *International Musicological Society: Report of the Twelfth Congress, Berkeley, 1977,* ed. Daniel Heartz and Bonnie Wade (Kassel, 1981), pp. 550-69.
[10]Michael Steinberg, "Introduction to Concerts in the Mass Media as a Means of Overcoming Cultural Barriers," in *Report of the Twelfth Congress,* pp. 561-63; the citation is from p. 562.
[11]Bailey, "The Decision to Publish: Economic Factors," p. 19.

conceived, is a broad and encompassing discipline; it is, more than anything else, a mode of thought whose domain is the real world of real art. If we insist on over-specializing, on treating smaller and smaller details of less and less significance at greater and greater length, we turn further and further in on ourselves. If, in our haste to achieve legitimacy with those we imagine to be our judges we consciously address an ever shrinking public, consciously increase our distance from the well-educated musician, and dismiss as unimportant, unoriginal, or insignificant everything that does not meet demonstrably artificial standards of severity, we shall have meaning only for ourselves. If we do all this, no matter how much we will have published, we already will have perished.

Teaching Music History in
Different Environments
Anne V. Hallmark

With the premise that academia today is commonly an uncongenial milieu; that many of us in musicology cannot find jobs and may eventually go elsewhere; or are struggling to hold on to undesirable jobs; or have jobs that require too much of us on too many fronts; or find after years of planning and building that programs are being cut from under us and that our dreams must be shrunk—it seems neither trivial nor presumptuous to examine some fundamental questions about the job we do and the field of which we are a part.

Anne V. Hallmark is chairman of the Department of Musicology at the New England Conservatory. Her edition of the complete works of Johannes Ciconia, edited with Margaret Bent, is soon to appear.

My experiences as a teacher of music history at three fundamentally different kinds of educational institutions prompt me to address the area of teaching, that realm where we try to communicate our knowledge, our curiosity, our prejudices even, to those who presumably know less than we. This is fundamentally different from addressing our colleagues within the field: there we speak to each other (at least ideally) as specialists on common ground. To teach students requires that we clarify what we know so that it will be meaningful to someone without our previous knowledge and insight.

The focus will be specifically on undergraduate teaching, and on teaching music as history, that is, within a broader historical framework—a luxury for most of us, given the ubiquitous "Introduction to Music," "Music Appreciation," and "Concepts of Music" courses that we teach. It will become clear as the paper progresses that the bias is toward a unified aim, though environment may vary; while method and techniques may differ, the goals need not. I lay no claim to special expertise in this subject. I do not presume to offer advice, but rather to ask a number of provocative questions.

The challenges which face our field seem to be multiplying, though other generations have no doubt faced similar or equal challenges. Among the fundamental questions: Will music and music history survive in college curricula of the future? Will music history continue to have a place within the realm of the humanities, and be seen as a valuable intellectual pursuit? Or will music in our age of new austerity be seen as an inessential frill? Have we contributed to this image, and can we counter it?

The institutions where I have taught all give genuine support to the study of music, though the nature of that support differs considerably from one place to another. At Vassar College, with only an undergraduate program but an excellent and diverse faculty and wonderful facilities (for example, each listening room has its own scores, recordings, and piano), students tend to have a broad cultural background. They understand and are curious about inter-connections of things, about concepts of history and culture. The greatest unevenness occurs in specific musical training, in performance or analysis; and sometimes Vassar students could properly be accused of dilettantism.

Massachusetts Institute of Technology students, on the other hand, tend to be very strong on analytical skills, and have curiosity about "how music works." They are frequently spectacular in counterpoint. In teaching such students, I encounter a lack of historical sympathy or understanding; and often the insight into the subjective and creative aspect of music is severely limited.

At New England Conservatory, the students tend to be intensely curious on all levels—historical, analytical, emotional; and these are the students from whom one can expect most in terms of previous (and simultaneous) musical training. As a group they are weakest in historical understanding, critical thinking, and in insight on broad cultural issues. Not infrequently those who are the most talented have the least time for classroom studies because they are constantly under pressure from playing engagements and competitions. The least bright Conservatory students tend to be considerably less intelligent than those of the other two institutions—sometimes they are naturally gifted players with little intellectual bent, sometimes narrow technicians without curiosity beyond their own instruments or repertoire, who feel their time best spent in the practice room. But the best are a joy, and this is true in the other institutions as well.

You may well ask whether these students—if accurately described— have such traits by nature or by acquisition, that is, whether the curricula have shaped their musical personalities. I would answer that while shaping certainly continues, these descriptions are of biases and talents which the students usually have upon entering such institutions. The programs of each do not offset these basic tendencies in any of the places mentioned; and this is not a comment on the strength or weakness of specific courses of study. The environment of each institution as a whole, and attitudes of faculties as a whole, are significant in shaping attitudes. At Vassar music prospers because of its honored place within the liberal arts, within the humanities; music has long been seen by the college as a valuable intellectual pursuit. Performing, on the other hand, while given strong support, is part of a much younger tradition there; credit for performance was not always given, and this reflects an attitude not unlike many liberal arts institutions. The attitude has changed, but the tradition lingers.

MIT's tradition, of course, is quite different, and one sees vividly there the sometimes uneasy alliance of the sciences and humanities. The facilities for music are good—for example, the library's collection of scores and research materials is excellent (one of Boston's best kept secrets); and there are ample opportunities for music-making, within large ensembles and chamber groups as well. The scene is a lively one, and the performance-level high. The attitude of the MIT administration is that only the best (in any area) will do for their students, and that they have a responsibility to provide students with a broad-based education. This is certainly laudable. Difficulty arises, however, when priorites are considered. Science and engineering reign at MIT, and no amount of lip service to a liberal tradition can disguise that fact. Music is often considered an "essential frill," and those who are contemptuous of a course like "Physics for Poets" cannot understand a historian's reluctance to teach "Medieval Music for Engineers."

History and the liberal arts also play a secondary role at the New England Conservatory, but attitudes are quite different: music history especially can escape the "frill" category. In the role of music historian, I have frankly found myself filling a more essential role at the Conservatory than at any other place: by facing the challenge of proving why history is essential to performers, one is rewarded by extensive response. Not all of it is enthusiastic, but that is part of the challenge, and at least the issue is being engaged. The Conservatory's difficulties are again different from the other institutions. Faced with a kind of education more expensive than most, with a one-to-one teacher-student ratio at the core of the program, the school has often made compromises in other teaching areas. Classroom courses in music history are only recently below forty students as a norm; history teachers are responsible for teaching six courses per semester, though by special arrangements the loads are reduced to four. These difficulties put strain on teacher and student alike.

Music teaching in some form will survive in these institutions as long as they remain open. The issue of how valued music is within the curriculum is neither a new issue nor one with standard answers. But I for one have become convinced that one can and should teach all students with the same fundamental goals in mind, regardless of what we think their involvement with music will be, or what their biases are. A primary role for us as music historians is to be persuasive about the value of our subject.

Ambivalence about music in our institutions might be seen as a mirror of the ambiguous attitudes of society itself, and toward art music in particular. Music's power is such that it is a fundamental part of nearly all cultures, but we are not surprised when men disagree about *which* music gives pleasure: consider that many of Beethoven's later works were still being regarded as "crazy" in the early decades of this century; consider the contempt in which Debussy was held by the French academy; or the defensive proselytizing Tovey felt was necessary in regard to Mozart; or the reactions to the *Altenberg Lieder* first performance. One can find similar attitudes in our own day: a leading American composer wrote an article in which he asked, "Who Cares If You Listen?"; we are besieged on all sides by other people's music, and, what is far worse, aurally invaded by Muzak in supermarkets, airplanes, and elevators. At the same time, recordings have made music more widely accessible than ever before (regardless of how positively one views this trend), and the technical proficiency of today's performing organizations is generally higher than it was 150 years ago, if we can believe the reports of Schumann and Berlioz. What hope do we have of channeling such power, diversity, and controversy in the classroom? To put it another way—is it possible for us to make this vital subject completely irrelevant?

As a kind of answer to that question I would like to suggest a distinction between technical and historical understanding. In teaching music history, we should not be vague about our aims (which imply method) and methods (which reflect aims). As one scholar phrases it, we must first provide orientation in the special discourse of our discipline.[1] This orientation is in essence technical, though it may quickly and continuously lead outward to so-called liberal realms. With this orientation a student acquires skills and sophistication of a quantifiable and cumulative sort; for us as educators, issues and arguments come when determining which skills are important, in determining whether traditional pedagogical methods will be used or abandoned. I doubt I am being controversial in saying that to be knowledgeable in music a student must understand and be able to hear a V - I cadence or a *forme fixe*. Knowledge is lacking if he or she can discuss the significance of tonality in the eighteenth century but not hear a modulation to the dominant. To be able to listen critically, and to be able to articulate the language of music, should be fundamental and unalterable aims for our students. Teaching these skills is necessary at every level, but it is not the exclusive domain of music historians. We should neither avoid teaching such skills nor focus too much on them; in doing the latter, we fail to communicate what *is* our domain, the teaching of historical understanding regarding music.

Before discussing this, let me say the following. I am anxious not to make comparative judgments about music history versus theory or performance or composition, but to stress the value of the music-historical approach. In so doing, it is hoped that this will add to dialogues with our colleagues in music who are not primarily historians. A defensive posture may lead to excessive or unquestioning reliance on inherited traditions or to a condition where communication with non-historian colleagues is limited to occasional rhetorical sniping. Is it not better to indulge in impassioned argument on a continuous basis, respecting each other even as we pound the table in frustration?

The music historian does not take the finished or single composition as his or her only grounding, except as it provides the basis for teaching

---

[1]Russell Bostert, "Teaching History," *Scholars Who Teach,* ed. Steven M. Cahn (Chicago, 1978), 14.

the language of music. His or her realm is the delicious ambiguity surrounding composition—for example, biography, influences, source studies, performing practice, aesthetics, and criticism—and the study of its history and environment, involving, as Eggebrecht says in *The New Grove,* "a critical interpretation of sources and a demonstration of connections between non-contemporaneous events."[2] This area, it seems to me, is not hierarchical or cumulative. At least some of its value lies in challenging the imagination, in creating or increasing curiosity, in questioning standard assumptions or values, and in harnessing curiosity toward demonstrable problems even though these may not have unambiguous solutions. Let me offer some examples of this point from performing practice.

The performance of Bach's B-Minor Mass under the direction of Joshua Rifkin,[3] controversial as it is, directly links historical insight, research, and reconstruction with performance. Not only the size of the ensemble (which shocked many), but also the kinds of instruments and bows and bowing techniques, not to mention tempo, ornamentation, and tuning, affected the sound of the performance and the listener's perception of it. How different from Richter's recording, even Harnoncourt's! Fundamental musical and historical questions are raised in considering the differences, and these differences should be explored not only in the press and among musicologists but in the classroom. Likewise revealing are comparisons between Safford Cape and David Munrow (or Thomas Binkley, or Konrad Ruhland) in their early-music performances. Each performer shows not only a strong musical identity, food for thought and argument in itself, but also a dependence on the historical resources of his own generation, and the listener is enlightened by considering the resources as well as the finished product.

[2]"Historiography," *The New Grove Dictionary of Music and Musicians,* ed. Stanley Sadie (London, 1980), VIII, 593.
[3]Boston, November 1981, and New York, January 1982 (to be available as a recording); see Nicholas Kenyon's review of the Boston performance and of Rifkin's paper in support of his performing forces (*The New Yorker,* 14 December 1981, 189-98) and Andrew Porter's brief comment on the New York performance (ibid., 18 January 1982, 119).

How do we react to multiple versions of a work, as with *Don Carlos,* or to revised versions of a work, as with Schumann's D-Minor Symphony? Does it matter that the *Lyric Suite* last movement is found to be full of personal allusions? Are Machaut chansons intended to be performed by voices alone? For me as a historian it matters on many levels that Haydn and Mozart influenced one another; that Richard Muhlfeld inspired Brahms to write his Clarinet Quintet; that Ferrara provided a rich environment for composers and performers in the 15th and 16th centuries, and that the Archbishop of Salzburg did not in the 1770s; that the term "Renaissance" may not be the best or only description for a period in Western European music history; or that *basso continuo* as a label for the Baroque era may blind us to other developments and discontinuity; that chant in the early Middle Ages may not have been sung in uniform rhythmic values. It also matters that important aspects of Wolf's biography were suppressed for many years; that only now are we acquiring a collected edition of Wagner; that Goethe preferred Zelter's songs to Schubert's.

The exploration of any one of these areas may not yield information or concepts relevant to any other, nor will such exploration lead to answers in any quantifiable sense. On the contrary, exploration can reveal such complexity that a teacher's task is often greater than before; one must not retreat in the face of open-endedness or bottomlessness, but use all one's resources to help a student create order without accepting simplicity. The insights that may be provided lead back to music and also outward to larger historical issues or larger educational issues. Surely this is sufficient justification for including music history among the fit pursuits of higher education.

Our success in teaching, it seems to me, depends on a mixture of these two fundamentally different areas outlined above. Technical and liberal, specific and general, quantitative and qualitative, certain and ambiguous—these may not be the best terms to apply to each area, complex as each is in its own way, but the point remains that to distinguish between them enables us to see a unified aim more clearly in the end. Teaching which fails on either side cannot be said to represent music history at its best.

In an essay of Alfred North Whitehead one finds a worthwhile clarification of some ideas I suspect are implicit in our teaching but largely intuitive for most of us. In his "The Rhythm of Education," Whitehead sets forth three stages of intellectual progress—stages of romance, of precision, and of generalization—and advocates their recognition and use in teaching. In the stage of romance, "The subject has the vividness of novelty; it holds within itself unexplored connections with possibilities half-disclosed by glimpses and half-concealed by the wealth of material. In this stage knowledge is not dominated by systematic procedure."[4] No child, no student is prepared for tasks ahead in learning without this stage, and in self-education the necessity for this first stage is particularly evident: learning does not occur without it. Many adults cannot imagine taking the time or energy to master Rubik's Cube or Dungeons and Dragons, but I suggest that many young people are powerfully drawn to the mystery of them, and can appreciate the "half-disclosed," "half-concealed" possibilities they provide. The ground is thus prepared for the stage of precision, where facts must be mastered in systematic order, where grammar is learned, where exactness of formulation is required. Whitehead stresses that "a stage of precision is barren without a previous stage of romance; unless there are facts which have already been vaguely apprehended in their broad generality, the previous analysis is an analysis of nothing."[5]

The final stage—of generalization—is like Hegel's synthesis: as Whitehead states, "a return to romanticism with added advantage of classified ideas and relevant technique. It is the fruition which has been the goal of the precise training. It is the final success."[6] Here is where the larger results of detailed problem-solving can be seen to be fruitful, as long as a student is guided to larger horizons. Two examples from my own experience suggest themselves. At an early age and for a brief while I had the dubious pleasure of studying piano with the village piano teacher. Not only was she short on romance (though long on precision),

---

[4]Alfred North Whitehead, "The Rhythm of Education" (London, 1922), reprt. in *The Aims of Education* (New York, 1929), 28-29.
[5]Whitehead, 29.
[6]Whitehead, 30.

but I am convinced that her failure to teach me anything of the relationship between C major and G major, to name but one instance, revealed a pronounced lack of any generalized understanding. Conversely, a seminar in graduate school on "Byzantine Alleluias of the Fourth Mode" explored the mainly uncharted relations between Eastern and Western chant by focusing on the transmission of a small, unified, and promising sample. An obvious reason for the success of this course was that its narrowness was chosen not randomly, in hopes of finding something beyond itself, but deliberately, by a teacher and scholar who had long before passed into the stage of generalization in the subject.

The Polish author Czeslaw Milosz illuminates these stages, it seems to me, in his poem "Readings":

> You asked me what is the good of reading the Gospels in Greek.
> I answer that it is proper that we move our finger
> Along letters more enduring than those carved in stone,
> And that, slowly pronouncing each syllable,
> We discover the true dignity of speech.
> Compelled to be attentive we shall think of that epoch
> No more distant than yesterday, though the heads of Caesars
> On coins are different today . . .[7]

In his rich language and thought, Milosz demonstrates the complex interaction of romance, precision, and generalization, as well as their separate identities. Whitehead stresses in his discussion that "education should consist in a continual repetition of [the] cycle [of these three stages]," even within the same lesson. Difficult as this may be to attain, it seems a worthy aim. Some years ago, in a subsequently published lecture, Edward Cone used the Brahms Intermezzo, opus 118, no. 1, to demonstrate three stages in musical perception, equating such stages

[7]*Bells in Winter* (New York, 1978), 10.

with successive reactions to a mystery novel.[8]   I) One hears the piece (or reads the mystery) without knowing its outcome, with expectation created as and only as the work progresses; II) on second hearing (or reading), aware of the outcome but also of deliberate ambiguities and pleasures, one searches for and is preoccupied by specific details and characterizations; III) on third hearing one works to reconcile the realities of the first two, that is, to integrate the dramatic expectation of the first with the detailed knowledge provided by the second. Cone's lecture seems not only a recreation of Whitehead's stages, but also a multi-leveled demonstration of how one can include all stages in a single lecture.

Numerous instances suggest themselves from within an historical framework. For example, the romance of the medieval troubadours and trouvères can be presented by focusing on the composer/performer, the role of wandering musicians in medieval Europe, the haziness of the historical record. Precision enters by looking in detail at, for example, the troubadour song, "A l'entrada del tens clar," by studying through ear and eye or ear alone the melodic shape (with its difficulties), possible rhythmic shapes, and text-music relations. Though atypical for its repertoire, it is nonetheless useful provided that the norm can be demonstrated. Study of it can touch on specific and general questions related to rhythmic practice, accompaniment and ornament, manuscript transmission and—in this case—connections to another repertoire, since "A l'entrada" shares its melody with the Notre Dame conductus "Veris ad imperia." Equally interesting is the problem of the melody and mode: did the scribe miscopy the second half?

Mozart's *Musical Joke* might provide the basis for an effective discussion. Sufficient romance is probably provided by playing or listening to the work or a portion of it, though one can set the stage, as William Kirby suggests,[9] by describing Mozart's sense of humor in his letters and conversation. The piece's vocabulary is, in its straight-

---

[8]Edward T. Cone, "Three Ways of Reading a Detective Story—or a Brahms Intermezzo," *Georgia Review* 31 (1977), 554-74.
[9]*Music in the Classic Period: An Anthology with Commentary* (New York, 1979), 519.

forward moments, a kind of model for eighteenth-century phrase structure, melodic contour, and tonality: these can be addressed in advance of discussing its humor. But the humor of it is wonderfully instructive concerning expectation, and not only leads back to detailed issues of eighteenth-century musical language and Mozart's awareness of the role of expectation, but also outward to unanswerable questions: why is it funny? Can one distinguish between this and a badly written piece? How much of our "appreciation"of a work depends on knowing who wrote it? Other examples of humor could be cited or played, Haydn's "Joke Rondo," for instance. On the other hand, a comparison with *Eine Kleine Nachtmusik,* as Einstein suggested, gives an example of "how Mozart did it right."

The examples above have focused on specific works; one could point to larger topics like three-key areas in Schubert, or Bach's synthesis of French and Italian styles, or Webern's perspective on Isaac, or the role of program in nineteenth-century music. Time in the classroom is of course an issue: would that we could follow Gustave Reese's example in his graduate seminars, where classes went on, I am told, until he was finished. How do we decide how to spend the limited time we have for a course, given all the constraints of class size and varied student background, given the problems of requiring outside listening? There is so little time that one is often frustrated with trying to integrate material; sometimes I feel I go on to generalizing without enough precision, at the expense of a solid understanding of the music. The problem is inordinately complicated when, as often happens, students with little background find the integration simpler to understand on a superficial level, and work hard at avoiding involvement with scores and musical details.

Many other questions—philosophical and practical—need to be asked. To what extent should we be concerned in teaching the sociological side of music history? Should the philosophical assumptions of our discipline be explicitly addressed in graduate training? What schools of thought exist with regard to teaching music history, and how do the textbooks we use affect our approach? Have we slid into a "reactive role" in our teaching, as one scholar puts it, where we react to the pressure of the moment, the fashion of the day? Similarly, can we escape the charge of "hucksterism"? The pressure caused by current levels of unemployment among musicology Ph.D.s, problems of tenure, and declining enrollments for courses and programs is severe, making the preceding two questions especially timely.[10]

At the center, however, it seems to me, is the question articulated by Kerman and Lowinsky in 1964-65.[11] Do we teach music as a window onto society, or do we teach so that, as Kerman says, "men in society are studied as a means of furthering the comprehension of works of art?"[12] The scope of this essay permits no more than the asking of these questions.

In closing let me turn to a historian's elegant statement regarding the impossibility of consensus in what we do:

> Historians and non-historians, teachers and students alike, should rejoice that there is no royal road to understanding the past, or to teaching those who become interested in it. There is no [single] structure of underlying principles; there are no basic laws. Let historians, at least, not be ashamed to admit this. Let them be proud to proclaim it and to teach it. Their students will not suffer from its recognition, since the intellectual discipline of properly studying the past has its own built-in relevance. For every intellectual explanation of human experience, whatever its special mode of inquiry, must rely on history for its content. There is no alternative.[13]

[10]Other essays in *Scholars Who Teach* also deal sensitively with these questions and problems. See also *The New Liberal Arts: An Exchange of Views,* ed. James D. Koerner (New York: Alfred P. Sloan Foundation, 1981). In the field of music, some of the most illuminating writing has been done by Cone, Meyer, and Sessions. See, for example, Edward T. Cone, *Musical Form and Musical Performance* (New York, 1968); Leonard Meyer, *Emotion and Meaning in Music* (Chicago, 1956), and *Music, The Arts, and Ideas* (Chicago, 1967); Roger Sessions, *The Musical Experience of Composer, Performer, Listener* (Princeton, 1950).
[11]Joseph Kerman, "A Profile for American Musicology," *Journal of the American Musicological Society* 18 (1965), 61-69; Edward Lowinsky, "Character and Purposes of American Musicology; a Reply to Joseph Kerman," ibid. 18 (1965), 222-34; Kerman, Communication, ibid. 19 (1965), 426-27.
[12]"A Profile," 62.
[13]Bostert, 29.

Musicology and Criticism

Rose Rosengard Subotnik

The task with which I have been charged here is to address the situation of scholarship in non-traditional areas of musicology. Given the limitations of space and of my experience, I shall focus here on the character and problems of an area in which I myself have worked, that of scholarly music criticism.

Defining this field is itself a problem, especially if one tries to do so through reference to existing American scholarship; for outside of

Rose Rosengard Subotnik is a scholar and writer of serious music criticism. Her articles on Adorno's criticism have appeared in the *Journal of the American Musicological Society* and in *19th-Century Music*. See "Adorno's Diagnosis of Beethoven's Late Style: Early Symptom of a Fatal Condition," *Journal of the American Musicological Society* 29 (1976), 242-75; and "The Historical Structure: Adorno's 'French' Model for the Criticism of Nineteenth-Century Music, *19th-Century Music* 2 (1978), 36-60.

journalistic criticism, which is not my concern here, American music criticism is an elusive and fragmentary phenomenon. For the most part it consists in scattered, highly divergent essays by individual scholars who seldom identify their enterprise as criticism, and who work in relative isolation, since there is rarely more than one such figure in any American music department, since few of their students can afford to remain in criticism, and since few, if any, have generated even a small, identifiable school of critical methods or thought. A handful of these scholars are well known and publicly admired, or at least respected, by their more traditional colleagues, although I have observed that even prominent scholars are subject to surprisingly widespread private disapproval, in traditionalist circles, for the non-factual nature of their critical works, or else are principally esteemed for those aspects of their work that fall within the domain of traditional empiricist scholarship. Relatively few critical works—and I include here even Charles Rosen's *The Classical Style* and Joseph Kerman's study of the Beethoven quartets, despite the unavoidable use of these books in historical survey courses—have had a major role in defining the activities, goals, or attitudes of American graduate programs in musicology. Instead of being integrated into the very core of musicological study, the methods and viewpoints of critical scholars seem to be subjected to deep analysis mainly in relatively unconventional courses that carry little weight in the student's preparation for doctoral exams.

And just as the critical works of even such leading American musical scholars as Rosen, Kerman, Meyer, Cone, Treitler, and Lippman, not to mention those of such non-Americans as Dalhaus and Nattiez or such non-musicologists as E. D. Hirsch, Roland Barthes, or Harold Bloom, have individually exerted far less influence than it seems to me they should, so too, collectively they have had relatively little impact on the character and direction of American musicology as an institutional whole. Unlike its counterparts in literature and the visual arts, American musicology has yet to devote any substantial energy or support either to the intellectual issues of criticism or to the definition and study of any extant body of critical investigation or theory. On the whole, in fact, the study of critical literature is openly deprecated by mainstream musicology as a purely derivative and parasitical enterprise, even though for years, now, it has dominated curricula in English literature at most American universities. I myself have encountered strong resistance on just such grounds to the very idea of making Adorno's musical writing an object of serious scholarship, again notwithstanding the fact that Adorno's criticism has affected European musicology profoundly. One established traditionalist actually explained his resistance to my work (which he confessed to not knowing well) and also that of some far better known critical scholars by saying simply "I don't like the category."

Criticism, including the study of criticism, remains an unestablished field of musical scholarship. In part, I would say, this very status, which impedes the definition of criticism, constitutes evidence of intellectual attitudes within the mainstream of American musicology that are restrictive, even to the point of being exclusionary. In fact, I would argue that the tenuous status of criticism reflects in no small measure the stifling effect that such attitudes, operating in positions of power, have on freedom of speech within American musicology as a whole. I shall return to these matters a bit later. In part, however, it must also be admitted that disunity of character and aims is implicit in *all* modern criticism, and that modern criticism by its very nature resists most definitive generalizations. For one general assertion that *does* seem to me valid is that modern criticism is an activity primarily concerned with the interpretation of meaning and, as such, depends heavily on the exercise of individual discretion for both its practice and its interpretation. Interpretation today, I believe, is largely an individualistic activity because it takes place in a world that no longer provides rational support for beliefs in any single set of principles, values, or conceptions of truth as a basis for universal understanding of one, single, unmistakable meaning. In brief, no particular interpretation of any human statement or artifact can be guaranteed by modern thought as universally valid, or, hence, as definitively correct.[1]

Whether or not interpretation has everywhere and always been subject to as much individual variance as is evident today is a matter I cannot take up here. What is more to the point is that the very need for interpretation seems, at least in the Western world, to be a distinctly modern phenomenon, and that in fact criticism in the West has always been primarily concerned with interpretation. It became so, according to Charles Rosen in the first of his two articles on Walter Benjamin, only toward the end of the eighteenth century.[2] Prior to this, criticism was principally concerned with judging value. Neither the nature of this change nor the time in which it occurred should surprise the student of history. Judging the value of the artifact presupposes that the meaning of that artifact has been unmistakably understood. Now in theory, at least, it was possible to assume an intended meaning as self-evidence and to pursue judgment in a spirit of confidence so long as Western culture was dominated, as it was during the Enlightenment, by a belief in abstract universal reason as a real and existing standard for the shaping of intelligible languages and for the determination of validity and truth.

[1] I agree with those scholars who argue that not even an originating artist's interpretation of his own work is epistemologically definitive or, for that matter, necessarily privileged. See Richard Taruskin's essay on performance in the present volume, and compare Charles Rosen's assertion that "not even the author's own exegesis can ever attach itself permanently to [a text], or pretend to be an integral or necessary condition of experiencing it" ("The Origins of Walter Benjamin," *New York Review of Books* 24, 10 November 1977, p. 37.) This viewpoint, prominent in current post-structuralist thought, is, to be sure, opposed by some of our most humane scholars, for example, E. D. Hirsch in *The Aims of Interpretation* (Chicago, 1976), chapter 5 (see also p. 7). On the whole I fear that in epistemological terms, Hirsch's argument rests on a kind of wishful thinking that overestimates the rationality of utterance, interpretation, and communication while underestimating the irreducibly individual or indeterminate aspects of such processes. At the same time, however, I do believe that a strong case can be made for the moral and epistemological value of trying to approximate, through a dialectical process, the original meaning of an utterance, so long as the ineradicable, and indeed, the governing roles of the interpreter's own consciousness in any act of interpretation is openly acknowledged. The value seems especially clear when the originator of an utterance is alive and available for questions.

[2] "The Ruins of Walter Benjamin," *New York Review of Books* 24 (27 October 1977), 32.

But as soon as universalistic conceptions of reason themselves became objects of criticism, as they did not only in the political activism of the French Revolution but also in Kant's philosophical critiques and, I would argue, in the more individualized works of Mozart and Beethoven, then confidence in judgments of value was bound to weaken. At the same time, an awareness was bound to grow of those differences in concrete individual experience and cultural values that limit the clarity with which an intended meaning can be communicated, especially as an artifact travels outside the circle of its origin, that is, of differences that turn the interpretation of meaning not into a parasitical diversion but into an urgent human need and also into a problematical process. One could say, into an art. And it was precisely at this historical juncture that great early modern thinkers began to describe the work of criticism as, in the words of Friedrich Schlegel, "itself a work of art," as well as to place the critical act, in Charles Rosen's words, "at the center of the work of art."[3] Even those modern twentieth-century idealists, such as Lévi-Strauss and Chomsky, who still hope to define new bases of universality within the domain of human thought, have been unable to validate the status of their principles or structures with scientific certainty.

Indeed, scientific certainty itself is an abstract Newtonian ideal of universality that has been undermined by the passing of the Enlightenment world-view and the growth of the modern critical spirit. The very rise to prominence of empirical research in nineteenth-century Western culture bears witness to the decline of Western belief in abstract scientific certainty since, as Hume pointed out during the Enlightenment itself, empirical observations cannot claim the same qualities of universality, necessity, and certainty as we impute to abstract mathematical laws. A truly consistent scientific empiricism,

---

[3]Ibid. For insight into this monumental upheaval in Western thought, as well as into the concomitant decline of Western ethnocentricity and the emergence of that relativistic outlook that produced modern criticism, there is still no better guide than Arthur O. Lovejoy's *The Great Chain of Being* (Cambridge, Mass., 1936), chapters 10 and 11.

that is, as opposed to an empiricism that has merely adopted uncritically the ideals of an earlier rationalism, must eventually take on a skeptical attitude toward universal principles and admit of limits on the scope and certainty of its own observations. Positivism, a nineteenth-century invention, has been a favored Western response to this pressure, though it is by no means the most humane, resilient, or enlightening one, least of all for twentieth-century problems, largely because beneath its radical reduction of knowledge to the empirical sphere, it has kept intact an inappropriate allegiance to an ideal of essentially absolute scientific certainty.

At any rate, by the early twentieth century, the limits to scientific certainty were marked quite literally by Heisenberg's formulation of the uncertainty principle. And today there is a growing tendency to view modern science, in its totality, much less as a source of universal values than as merely another cultural artifact, an artifact that is no doubt useful and "paradigmatic," to borrow Thomas Kuhn's term,[4] but also restricted in its validity by the limitations of actual experience, especially those amounting to the blind-spots of the particular culture that produced it. The uncritical conception of science as a privileged embodiment of universal truth is rejected even by thoughtful scientists, as a potential source of false claims and evil values.

In fact, the limits of scientific validity and certainty must be evident to *any* thoughtful observer of the modern technological world. And once these limits are acknowledged, one would expect serious attention to be given to new modes of thought, such as criticism, which question a wide range of traditional scientific concepts, from universal reason to scientific objectivity, and which might serve the modern spiritual recognition of relativism, including even its empiricist components, more honestly than do the absolute certainty and the confusion of ethnocentricity with universality that typified the Enlightenment. Yet as Morse Peckham suggested in *Beyond the Tragic Vision,* many Westerners, however modern in style or technology, continue to adhere

---

[4]Thomas S. Kuhn, *The Structure of Scientific Revolutions,* 2nd edn. (Chicago, 1970).

uncritically to a comforting Enlightenment belief in universal laws and certainty,[5] or at least, one might add, to some newer, thinly disguised, but essentially unchanged version of that belief.

I would argue that mainstream American musicology in its current state constitutes one such backwater. The ruling concept of knowledge within that mainstream seems to me to be shaped by an uncritical and outmoded notion of science, grounded on a dogmatic Enlightenment ideal of general laws and absolute verifiabilty, and overlaid with an accretion of equally dogmatic, though narrower and supposedly value-free or non-ideological, positivistic reverence for the so-called "hard" certainty of empirical fact.[6] And mainstream American musicology has found it easy to dismiss or reject criticism as a significant scholarly activity largely, I believe, because it judges criticism by this notion, even though, as Charles Seeger indicated some twenty years ago, in the *Journal of the American Musicological Society,* criticism is in fundamental ways the polar opposite of traditional science.[7]

Criticism is, in fact, as many noted philosophers since Schlegel have observed, an essentially aesthetic undertaking, a counterpart to the work of art itself. As such, one would suppose it had great value as an instrument for dealing intellectually with music, especially the music of the past two centuries, which, in its own way, has been preoccupied with the same problems of communicating meaning and establishing value in a relativistic world as criticism has been. But there can be no denying that when measured against old-fashioned scientific standards of

[5]Morse Peckham, *Beyond the Tragic Vision* (New York, 1962), p. 76.
[6]It is the presence of this scientific ideology that accounts for the "modernist" character of what Richard Taruskin terms the "reconstructionist" attitude, the very attitude that has established itself as traditional in what I call "mainstream" musicology. Taruskin is certainly right to identify Hanslick as the point of departure for current American musicological thought, though I would view Hanslick's philosophy not as an "astonishing" precursor of Stravinsky's but as part of the same cultural configuration that led to the prominence of positivism, empirical science, and industrial technology well within the nineteenth century. See also below, n. 10, on ideology and "non-ideology."
[7]Charles L. Seeger, "On the Moods of a Music-Logic," *Journal of the American Musicological Society* 13 (1960), 224-61; see particularly pp. 258-61.

absolute certainty and universal validity, or even against the alleged "hardness" of empirical fact, criticism, like composition itself, can be denigrated as a "soft" or flabby variety of thinking.

Let me dwell a bit on the relations of criticism first to empirical fact-finding and then to more general aspects of the traditional scientific ideal. That the empirical establishment of facts does not bring about any absolute state of knowledge should be clear, if not from Hume's testimony, then at least from the endlessness of the revisions with which we torment our factual textbooks. Even the most authoritative critical score has no absolute way of protecting every one of its crotchets and quavers from future empirical revisions. Still, there is a degree to which empirical studies can be reasonably, though roughly, measured through reference to the current status of fact. Criticism, however, largely eludes even such approximate measures of truthfulness; for expertise in criticism consists not in the mastery of any body of facts but in the refinement of an unquantifiable sensibility. The domain of criticism, moreover, is huge, potentially encompassing all of human experience and thought, for there is scarcely a culture, or discipline, or body of artifacts from which the conscientious critic cannot derive means for refining his sensibility further. Mastering even a small portion of such a domain is quite obviously the work of a lifetime, during which the critic will have far less opportunity than the specialized empiricist to work up facts from scratch or to certify them as up-to-date.

But let us assume that the good critic pays meticulous attention to ongoing empirical research, so that by current standards of information, he is able to avoid at least significant error. Even in this best possible case, the domain staked out by the critic will still contain, at the close of his career, far more messy variables, unknowns, and even unknowables than the severely restricted domain of his empiricist counterpart, and will be far more openly permeated by speculation. This is because criticism is not primarily concerned with elements, conclusions, or kinds of knowledge that can be characterized fairly by the traditional "hard" scientific choice of right or wrong. Being inherently relativistic, criticism admits its inability to achieve scientifically definitive results or to protect its findings against the hazard—a hazard shared, I insist, by many facts—arising from differences or changes in scholarly sensibility. In this respect he differs sharply from the traditionalist. Whereas the traditionalist may admit that the "facts" of a modern critical edition could someday be challenged, he can scarcely imagine that the very *idea* of such an edition might be dismissed or rejected, by some future culture, as an ideal of significant knowledge. The critic, by contrast, must grapple from the outset with the notion of a time or place in which not only his dates but also his interpretations of data and the ideals of knowledge underlying his interpretations may be disregarded, or even ridiculed. (By and large the American critic already works in such a time and place.) In effect the critic, like the post-Heisenberg scientist but unlike the traditional Newtonian musicologist, has in some sense to acknowledge his own presence in his act of scholarship and thereby the limitations of pure objectivity and universal validity that are entailed in his results by his particular outlook and decisions. And finally, to complete the portrait of the modern critic as a post-Newtonian, the critic, or at least the fair-minded critic, is likely to distrust the unthinking use of accepted general principles, based on an uncritical belief in a self-efficient common sense and to treat the various objects of study as individualized problems of understanding, requiring constant adjustments in discretion and sensibility for fair treatment. For that matter, even the critic who is dogmatically committed to a particular ideological doctrine is forced constantly to clarify his relation to that doctrine, thereby giving his reader a fair chance to discern his commitment.

You may notice that I have so far emphasized the epistemological value of fairness over that of accuracy. This emphasis is of particular importance, I believe, when one goes beyond a mere description of criticism to a consideration of what constitutes good criticism. I do not claim that the good critic can or should be liberated from either a reasonable respect for facts or a healthy repugnance for factual distortion. I do not advocate giving license to self-indulgent fantasies of free association among critics or releasing the critic from the burdens of hard work and discipline. Nor do I think it advisable to try to free the critic from that adherence to rigorous principles of order which, as Stravinsky suggests so memorably in his *Poetics of Music,*[8] seem necessary even to the most imaginative intelligence.

What I do argue is that the kinds of hard work demanded by good criticism are different from those required by empirical research. What I do challenge is the inhuman demand that the critic master, *in their entirety,* not only the skills, literature, and problems of his own craft but also those of empiricist musicology as well as those of any other traditionally defined discipline on whose domain he treads, in order to assure his work a degree of certainty that is neither relevant to criticism nor intellectually attainable. What I do believe is that a diligent effort should be made to understand the critic's principles of order, along with the rationale and discipline based on those principles, on their own terms.

This last request, to be sure, involves problems, for the modern critic no longer has available an external set of supposedly true common principles from which to derive his own standards of rigor but must develop his principles of order from within his own thought. The same is true, of course, of the modern composer and even of the modern scientist, who in the last analysis must delimit the area, goals, and means of his research through personal convictions of propriety. This need to turn inward may make much of the modern critic's rationale difficult to fathom on first reading, and still more of it impossible to verify as generally valid.

In fact, it is difficult to deny that much of the value of the principles of order through which the good modern critic works out his ideas depends on an indefinable, though not imperceptible, quality of honesty that he brings to the development of those principles. This is why I emphasize the indispensability of fairness to the acquisition of human knowledge. The ultimate sources of the good modern critic's

[8]Igor Stravinsky, *Poetics of Music* (New York, 1960), Lesson III, "The Composition of Music," pp. 66-69.

principles of order, like those of the good modern composer or scientist, are not, I say, fully accessible to scientific demonstration, explanation, or validation precisely because honesty, which forms the foundation of those principles, is an essentially moral rather than scientific attitude. And for the perception of moral rigor, a capacity for fairness not only has power; it has far more power, I submit, than a capacity for accuracy.

Now, however much we may still be tied to an ideal of scientific universality, few in our profession are any longer comfortable with the notion of moral universals. I think most people today, outside the so-called "moral majority," would admit that even a principle as basic as "thou shalt not kill" admits of diverse sincere interpretations. In other words, we admit that the development of moral principles of order depends more upon the exercise of individualized discretion than upon recourse to what I called earlier "an external set of supposedly true common principles." The closest any of us can come to a universal mode in developing our moral rules as a basis of order is, as Kant suggested in his categorical imperative, by deriving those rules from a strong inner feeling of what ought to be universally binding. But this feeling does not in fact render our own rules universally binding or even acceptable. Remember that it was Kant himself, more perhaps than any other single Western individual, who (in spite of himself) sharpened the modern capacity to appreciate differences in moral imperative among individuals and cultures.

What all this leads to is the following argument. Just as the most authentic modern critic, composer, and scientist derives his essential principles of order from an underlying moral sense of what constitutes true and necessary coherence, trying with scrupulous good faith, like Beethoven in his sketchbooks, to work out those principles consistently and intelligibly, so as to establish what seems to him their general validity, so too, the authentic interpreter of modern criticism, or of *any* modern expression, ought to approach his material in a spirit of refined moral sensibiity. By this I mean that his own acts of interpretation and judgment should be fashioned in accordance with his own highest sense of fairness, even as he admits that sense to have the limitations of individual discretion rather than the absolute status and certainty of universal reason or a God-given decree.

It is my strong conviction that in a world where the rationales of the individuals we encounter are often unfamiliar and obscure, every interpreter of human expression has a moral obligation to go about the work of interpretation in a spirit of scrupulous good faith. And it is likewise my conviction that fulfilment of this *moral* obligation works to the *intellectual* benefit of the interpreter because it puts him in an unexcelled position to understand what he interprets. Let me emphasize that I do not construe a spirit of scrupulous good faith as synonymous with an attitude of uncritical acceptance, any more than I equate good critical methods with a rejection of intellectual rigor. The good modern interpreter may well have to reject, and quite vigorously, a rationale that, once understood, seems openly evil. He has a right, indeed, an obligation, to point out factual errors as well as inconsistencies of argument, though I believe it is useful to distinguish between significant and insignificant factual errors. And at no time must such an interpreter feel obliged to agree with either the premises or the conclusions of the work he studies. Nevertheless, I do believe that the modern interpreter is morally bound to withhold judgment, above all negative judgment, until he has fulfilled his *primary* obligation as a good critic, which is to make sure he has come as close as possible to understanding the sources and terms of another person's argument, the precise meaning as well as the main thrust and the spirit of that argument, and by no means least, the positive values of that argument.

Thus I would argue that since all of us, whatever our ideology or specialty, function as critics with respect to each other's work, we ought to go about performing that function in a spirit of good faith and even generosity. We ought to bring to our interpretation of another man's expression at least a provisional assumption that the man has principles of rationality and order that give him reasons for saying precisely what he does. We ought to ask, wherever possible, for clarification of what we do not understand. We ought to bring enough interest and intellectual curiosity about another man's work to refrain from pointing out its weaknesses until we have absorbed whatever goodness it offers. We ought to bring the courage, another moral quality, to rely in our interpretations and judgments on a fair and honest, though always fragile, faculty of discretion, individualized to the case at hand, instead of on the unexamined authority of general rules which may be inappropriate or unreasonable.[9] We ought to bring to our interpretations a genuine conviction that views of knowledge or truth that differ from our own are not necessarily wrong, inferior, or negligible. And we ought to bring an acute awareness of the degree to which our own principles and values, from which we are never free, affect our understanding and evaluation of others, together with the flexibility and rigor to reexamine our own standards whenever they run up against the uncongenial. Attitudes like these, which might nurture a magnificent climate of free speech, have not, to my knowledge, been prominent in the response of traditionalist American musicology to most works of criticism, or to any non-conventional essays into methodology, theory, or cross-disciplinary research.

Of course, once the easy certainty of scientifically "hard" and general principles is relinquished, the understanding and evaluation of scholarly work, especially work in an unfamiliar mode, becomes fraught with risk. I would argue, however, that by refusing to risk an' exercise of discretion, American musicology faces far more serious risks, such as those of alienating many of its own most gifted students or prospective students, and of removing itself permanently from the mainstream of modern thought. (How many non-musicologist humanists, even those working on the history or theory of various arts, find it worth their time to attend our conventions or to read almost any

[9]Clearly I am advocating an extension of the sensibility underlying modern criticism to all of musicology. Thus, whereas Taruskin in effect associates the mainstream musicologist with a traditional scientific ideal, "the establishment of generalizing criteria," I would argue that *any* humanistic scholar is far closer to the artist in his activities, or, for that matter, to Taruskin's own model of the performer. In all three of the latter categories, I believe, works that can be fully accounted for through general principles are as limited in value as those that aim no higher than at "getting it right."

of our journals?) Worst of all, our field faces the risk of perpetuating many of the inhumane practices and values in society at large which stem from an outmoded worship of science and which a true humanistic discipline should be superbly equipped to counteract.

Even now, traditionalist resistance to the unconventional has already had some ill-effects so disturbing as to suggest other, less admirable motives for such resistance besides a simple, good-faith adherence to old-fashioned scientific ideals. I return here to the current status of free speech within American musicology. Free speech, after all, was an ideal that developed out of the same Enlightenment values as Newtonian scientific ideals. One would suppose that any true believer in the ultimacy of the latter would be up in arms about the slightest infringement on the former. Yet who in this Society would persuasively argue that American musicology today is characterized by a true state of free speech, that is, by a genuine hospitality to a diversity of ideologic viewpoints, and a determination if not to encourage then at least to protect the activities of those who dissent from the traditionalist ideology of non-ideology?[10] What counterpart does American musicology, in its various institutional forms, offer to a civil liberties union that would protect the unconventional among us from the silencing effects of insecurity with the unfamiliar, prejudice against whole "categories" of study, or just plain intellectual laziness within the traditionalist establishment?[11]

[10]As my conception of "ideology" aroused controversy during the presentation of this essay, it may be worth restating that conception. I think of ideology not, in positivistic fashion, as that unfortunate dogmatism which invalidates all intellectual achievements except those based on the non-ideological truth of Western science, but rather as that context of particular ideas and beliefs that define (and thereby shape and restrict) the mental domain of *all* human beings. I elaborated on this conception in a lecture given at the annual meeting of the Society for Ethnomusicology at Indiana University in 1980, entitled "The Role of Ideology in the Study of Western Music."

[11]Leonard Meyer, an open-minded scholar by any standard (at least in my judgment), has cautioned in response to this essay that the genuine right to freedom of speech must not be confused with the specious right to a platform or audience. And I would agree that no individual can automatically blame his failure to achieve publication or acceptance of a paper proposal on ideological prejudices rather than on his own inadequacy. But I would also argue for the converse: that incompetence ought not to be automatically accepted as the actual basis on which traditionalists deny the non-traditionalist a platform or professional footing, especially when there seems to be a pattern of ideological discrimination.

In fact free speech is no more simple and unproblematical an ideal in the relativistic, culturally diversified modern world than scientific or moral absolutism. To foster it in a spirit of genuine fairness has required constant shifts of sensibility, reapplications of discretion, and responsiveness to ever-new questions of individual merit. This is a messy process that holds out no promise of realizing definitive conclusions or even of formulating general laws that can cover every conceivable contingency. It is a process that has, in effect, forced fundamental reinterpretations of free speech itself as a less than self-evident or absolute value. All in all, this process does not fit well with traditional Western ideals of a clean, efficient scientific thoroughness. And yet there is, at least at present, no alternative to this messy application of discretion, in good faith, if the spirit of the ideal underlying free speech, the freedom to be individual, is to be maintained in the modern world.

And the situation is similar if the spirit of the ideal underlying traditionalist scientific conceptions, namely respect for truth, is to be maintained. Indeed, it is rarely, if ever, possible to maintain the spirit of any human value by maintaining uncritically old formulations of that value, even if the technological apparatus for reaffirming those formulations is modernized.[12] If the modernization of means is not itself self-critical, that is, if it does not derive from its own state of change a reformulation of the principles underlying it, then the progress represented by such modernization is merely cosmetic, and not humane. With respect to humane values, this sort of modernization is actually injurious, for it fails to confront significant changes in the circumstances and attitudes of the human world and, hence, to provide ways of securing humane values in a changed world.

[12]Again, I am in agreement with Taruskin, here with his suggestions that "any authentic, which is to say authoritative performance" must incorporate the sensibility of its performers and, indeed, that antiquarian attempts at presentation may well violate the eternal essence (not Taruskin's term) of an artwork. This same notion, that art is falsified by attempts to remove it from the temporal flux of the human condition, is one of T. W. Adorno's principal tenets. He takes it up explicitly with reference to performance practice in his essay "Bach Defended Against His Devotees," in *Prisms,* transl. Samuel and Shierry Weber (London, 1967), pp. 142-46.

Thus, in the case of scholarship, it no longer serves truth to presume the self-evidence and universal validity of one's own laws and values or to restrict the concept of knowledge to a determination of unarguable certainties, even if the abstract notion of absolute certainty is modified into a concrete notion of "hard" certainty, reinforced through ever more sophisticated empirical technologies. What is needed, in my judgment, to preserve the spirit of truth in a modern scholarly discipline, such as American musicology, is a recognition of genuinely pluralistic diversity as intrinsic not only to the enterprise of criticism but also to the modern conception of truth. Such recognition can only come about through a reassessment of current philosophies and policies, leading to a radical enlargement of sensibility and spirit, which in turn opens up and expands American musicology to dimensions far more worthy of it. Unless such a self-examination, painful though it be, is undertaken, mainstream American musicologists must expect to be viewed by many of their less conventional colleagues, including critics, as modern-day embodiments of that nineteenth-century anachronism, Beckmesser, who would rather chalk up divergences in expression, and call them errors, than listen for the beauty of an unfamiliar music.